D0282456

The One-Minute Scolding

The One- Minute Scolding

THE AMAZINGLY EFFECTIVE NEW APPROACH TO CHILD DISCIPLINE

Gerald E. Nelson, M.D.

Illustrations by Gertrud Mueller Nelson

SHAMBHALA PUBLICATIONS, INC.
1920 13th Street
Boulder, Colorado 80302

First Edition
Distributed in the United States by Random House and in
Canada by Random House of Canada Ltd.
Printed in the United States of America.

Library of Congress Cataloging in Publication Data
Nelson, Gerald E., 1933–
 The one-minute scolding.
 Bibliography: p.
 1. Discipline of children. I. Title. II. Title: Scolding : the
amazingly effective new approach to child discipline.
HQ770.4.N44   1984   649'.64   83-18410
ISBN 0-87773-260-4
ISBN 0-394-53661-4 (Random House)
ISBN 0-87773-272-8 (pbk.)
ISBN 0-394-72389-9 (Random House : pbk.)

Acknowledgements

Every book owes its existence to many persons. Deborah Stearns and Rusty Thorpe typed and retyped endless pages. Odette Filloux and Jacqueline Winterer carefully read the early manuscript and made many helpful suggestions.

I am especially grateful to Dennis Clark for his patient assistance and clear thinking and prodding me to "stay on task." I am grateful to Richard Lewak, my friend and partner, for his knowledgeable insights and wisdom and for helping me conceive and implement the "one-minute" concept. Lastly, I want to thank my wife, Gertrud, for her love, patience, and able assistance in writing the manuscript. Her illustrations capture the spirit of the book.

For the privacy of my patients, the examples I use in this book are composites or inventions with names and details changed and shuffled to make them unidentifiable. But it is to the children and parents in my practice that I am especially grateful. It is their acceptance and careful implementation of the One-Minute Scolding that gave flesh to the concept and thrilling hope for a solution to others.

Contents

Introduction

Good discipline is at the heart of the teaching process by which children learn how to function as happy and effective members of society. As such, discipline is one of the most important activities that can take place within a family. Yet, it is one of the most troublesome and least understood aspects of family life.

Our intent is not to fill the scholarly vacuum by addressing a technical study to our professional colleagues. On the contrary, we want to speak in plain language to all those frustrated parents, grandparents, teachers, and others who have accepted the responsibility of nurturing children. We have discovered an approach to discipline that is easy and really works. We call it *The One-Minute Scolding*.

So, before you put this book down, take a look at Chapter 8. If you recognize yourself or your children there, you have a problem. You also have a solution: *The One-Minute Scolding*.

1 About this Book

The One-Minute Scolding is a book about discipline—discipline that works. Its format is simple and it leaves both parent and child feeling good about themselves and each other. It tells the child clearly what rule has been broken and how the parent feels about the rule being broken. Yet it also tells the child that he is loved and cared for by the parent. Finally, it does what good discipline is supposed to do: it changes unwanted behavior, but even more, it teaches appropriate behavior. We call this disciplinary strategy the One-Minute Scolding.

Children like knowing how to behave. Correct behavior increases their sense of autonomy and security. Their good behavior and confidence also happens to please those around them. They are not against being agreeable and affording enjoyment to others. That feels good.

But appropriate behavior and reasonable choices don't always bloom naturally in children. Good behaviors are not "built in." They are learned. Discipline is one of the most important ways that parents teach behavior and impart values to their children. Discipline is a teaching tool, not a punishment.

Successful and happy discipline follows the child out of his home and into his wider world. As he grows, he is more and more secure in knowing how to act at school, on the playing field, or at his friend's house. His friends and his teachers appreciate him, his ability to express himself honestly and to handle disappointments, control his anger, and share his joys. He is welcomed because he wants to "play by the rules." His teacher is pleased and effective as she works with him because he knows how to listen, contribute, work, learn, and interact in the classroom. Our society is torn and troubled by people who have never learned how to behave by the rules or contribute positively. The rising rate of juvenile delinquency and crime exposes the difficulty parents face in teaching their children values and appropriate behaviors.

But does it help to blame parents? Most parents love their children and want to do their best in guiding and teaching them. Even at their best, parents have bouts with uncertainty and defeat. When stressed, any parent is tempted to reach backward in experience and reuse a disciplinary action from his or her own past. This is true even when parents acknowledge that the overall effect of their own childhood discipline was negative. Most parents realize that these "old-fashioned" disciplines won't work. They remember their feelings of sadness and anger if they were shamed and threatened into submission when they were children. Many parents know firsthand how fears and hurts have followed them into their adulthood as a result of caustic "put-downs," slaps, restrictions, or beatings. They remember far better the punishments than the "crimes." Now they feel the results of these experiences in fears, neurotic guilts, low self-esteem, lack of trust, and inability to risk. Parents don't want to repeat that for their own children.

One may argue the old punishments did work at one time. After all, they successfully suppressed unwanted behavior. But the price was too high. And what did they teach? Today, parents want an effective discipline that teaches good behavior, but even more, one that results in good warm relationships with their children. They want a discipline that allows the child to grow into a warm, trusting adult who relates well to others.

Because parents have given up on the "old-fashioned" ways, however, does not mean that they believe in some permissive approach that a few "authorities" espoused a decade or two ago. They do not want their children to run away with the power and tyrannize family and neighborhood with obnoxious, controlling behaviors that know no limits. Parents today know that discipline is absolutely necessary, but they are not at all certain what constitutes this "good discipline."

In our practice over the past ten years, we have worked with troubled children and their families. Some of these children were especially troubled and difficult because they had suffered multiple losses of parents and foster families. The more losses these children suffered, the more difficult they were to discipline. And the more difficult they were, the more they were passed from foster family to foster family, or from therapist to therapist. Everyone wanted to give up on them eventually, even though parents and therapists had taken them on initially with hope and love and positive feelings. We saw these children creating an endless and increasingly painful cycle of behaviors caused by loss and causing more loss. It was a tragically painful cycle that love and the best of intentions alone could not break for these children. The usual punishments and disciplines made little or no impact. Their inappropriate and even dangerous behaviors escalated to a point where their worst fear—abandonment—came true.

Everything we heard and saw pointed to the need for a whole new form of discipline. We felt that a new solution was called for especially in the cases of these children who were caught in the cycle of repeated poor behavior and repeated loss. Something had to break this cycle and repair the wounds. What kind of discipline could these children respond to?

The One-Minute Scolding arose out of that need. It was a strategy that worked so well for these very troubled children and their foster or adoptive parents that we began teaching it to parents who were single or divorced and whose children were struggling with loss. We taught it to teachers and mental health workers. We also began teaching it to parents of less troubled children and to parents of children who had no particular psychopathology. Its effectiveness was astonishing on a number of levels:

- The One-Minute Scolding changed the poor behavior of all kinds of children.
- The technique taught parents to be effective teachers of proper behavior and value.
- It strengthened that bond between mildly troubled children and their parents.
- It created a bond between children who had foster or adoptive parents. It repaired attachments.
- It left both parent and child feeling good about themselves and each other. Parents and children became stronger, happier people.

This is what discipline should produce and, with the

aid of this book, what you will achieve. The actual directions for the One-Minute Scolding are simple but the implementation takes practice. Read this book carefully and use it as a "hands-on" tool until you have mastered the technique.

This book shows you what the principles of the One-Minute Scolding are:

- It points out the unique character of its form.
- It shows you how it is good discipline and not a punishment.
- It discusses under what circumstances the scolding applies and guides you through the common difficulties.
- It shows you how to adapt the scolding to children of various ages and temperaments.
- It takes you through the process of how the scolding's sophisticated theory was developed.
- It explains how this scolding is an effective discipline for conscience development in all children.

2 The One-Minute Scolding

The One-Minute Scolding works because as effective discipline, it teaches. It is not a punishment that inflicts pain as a penalty for some offense. Punishment is not good discipline because it causes fear and anxiety in the child which actually inhibits learning.

The One-Minute Scolding provides a simple structure for the parent to discipline his child. It is really not all scolding. It has several parts:

- Scolding the behavior.
- A moment of transition.
- Positive reaffirmation of the child's worth.
- A quiz.
- A hug.

Look at the chart in this chapter. This is the skeletal structure of the One-Minute Scolding. The first part of the scolding is usually easy to remember. The parent touching or holding the child scolds the child for misbehavior when he breaks a household rule or fails to obey a significant order. The parent looks and acts as upset as she feels. She tells the child why she is scolding, explains the rule, and she continues until the child re-

The One-Minute Scolding

		Parent	Child	
TIME	**CONTENT**	**FEELINGS**	**FEELINGS**	**EXAMPLE**
30 seconds	Statement of parent's feeling addressing child's behavior	Annoyance Irritation Angry Furious Rageful Frustrated Worried	Worried Anxious Tense Scared Dread Terrified Tearful Sorry Remorseful	Parent: I am angry with you. You hit your sister. We don't hit in this house and I get very mad with you when you forget that rule. You hurt your sister and that's not the way to deal with your frustration. That makes me frustrated and very angry with you. You simply may not hit . . . etc.
ABRUPT CHANGE OF FEELING	**DEEP BREATH TRANSITION**		**ANTICIPATION**	Deep breath—a moment to change feeling tone:
30 seconds	Parent loving reaffirmation of child's worth	Warm Tender Gentle Caring Hopeful Confident Loving Nurturing Clear Certain Satisfied	Surprised Relieved Confused Pleased Remorseful Secure Loved Worthy Certain	You're such a neat fellow. I know you can do better. Sometimes you remember to be so loving to your sister. I love you. I want to be a mama for you. So you don't have to worry. Every time you forget the rule and hit your sister, I'll scold you. That will help you to remember.
Quiz				Why am I scolding you? Because I hit my sister. What will I do every time you forget? You're going to scold me. Why do I want to help you remember? You love me. You want to be a good mama. Come let's have a hug. Hug
Hug				

sponds with signs of feeling: a tear, a sad face, a quivering lip. The parent does not continue to scold past thirty seconds. (Very young or extrasensitive children require even less scolding time.)

> "Thomas! You hit your sister. We don't hit in this house. It makes me terribly angry when you hurt your sister. I've told you before and you forgot. That's no way for you to get what you want from her. It makes me angry, it hurts her, it solves nothing and that's just plain naughty behavior . . . " etc.

The transition period that follows the parent's expression of anger is very important. The parent pauses for a second, gets control of her feelings, reminds herself how much she loves her son, and then abruptly changes her approach. Her entire attitude is changed. Suddenly, an angry, scolding mother switches to a loving, nurturing mother.

Initially, the second half of the scolding is the more difficult to produce. Even though she has been very upset and angry, maybe even rageful, the parent must reassure the child of his worth. The child needs to know beyond a doubt that he is loved, that he will not be abandoned, that he is capable of changing and learning how to behave, and that he will be helped consistently. Everything about the way the parent expresses confidence and tenderness is felt in tone of voice, body language, and touch:

"You're a neat, delightful fellow."

A positive statement is followed by a feeling statement about him:

"I love you so much!"

And the child hears how he'll be able to behave properly:

"I'll help you. I want to be a good mama, so every time you forget and hit your sister, I'll scold you. Soon you'll remember that we don't hit. Even if you forget, I'll just keep reminding you. You're such a nifty brother and it's not necessary to forget . . . " etc.

The parent is reassuring, warm, and in control.

With this positive affirmation, most children feel relieved and reassured of their parents' love. Then the parent checks to see if she has been a clear and effective teacher with a quiz:

"Why am I scolding you now?"
"Because I hit my sister."

"Right!" Some praise rewards the child for knowing what this scolding is about.

"And why must I scold you every time you make a bad mistake?"

"Because I'm not supposed to hit my sister."

"Right! And because I love you so much! What are you supposed to do when you feel mad with your sister?"

"Come to you for help if I can't handle it."

"Right," etc.

The scolding ends with a hug, a symbolic and physical gesture that emphasizes the closeness of the relationship. The hug is primarily a message from the parent that the scolding lesson is ended. By accepting and returning the embrace, the child acknowledges the scolding as a loving gesture of the parent.

The One-Minute Scolding has a surprisingly simple structure and takes one minute of your time to administer, so it isn't time consuming. But within that simple structure, a powerful range of feeling is to be expressed and compressed.

However, to be angry with your child does not mean that you have stopped loving him. On the contrary, you probably wouldn't feel so angry if you didn't love him so much.

But it is easy for any of us to experience anger and love as mutually exclusive emotions. The parent feels this conflict of emotions. The child fears it. All of us have experienced the feeling of being banished to our rooms after having elicited the rage of an exasperated parent. The door is a heavy barrier between us and the rest of the family. Love is over and anger looms on both sides of the door.

Maurice Sendak, in his famous children's book, *Where the Wild Things Are*, lets us in on the monsters that rage and dance in the imagination of Max, who was sent to his room by his exasperated mother. Sendak also resolves the issue of where mother's love has gone by sending up dinner on the last page, and the dinner is still warm.

Max's monsters are powerful, but charming. Not every child's fear and anger gets tamed eventually. Nor is every child redeemed soon enough with an honest expression of love.

In the past when we disciplined a child for a misbehavior, we felt we weren't clear or effective unless we maintained a stance of disapproval over a long period of time—hours, or even days! Some parents felt that a child needed to remain uncomfortable for a long time in order to learn his or her lesson. But we know now that children learn quickly and we know that to remain disapproving of a child for a long time only diminishes that child's sense of his basic good nature. Feeling diminished interferes with the child's development as well as his capacity to behave well and to succeed.

Disapproving looks, the "silent treatment," or banishment from the scene create powerful feelings of rejection and abandonment in a child at precisely the moment that he needs to know that his parents are loving and strong enough to help him when he causes trouble. His fears of rejection and abandonment interfere with his learning the nature of his misbehavior or how he is to change the behavior. He is left only with feelings of fear, anger, and sadness.

So the One-Minute Scolding offers a transformative concept of discipline. Here anger and love are not allowed to be mutually exclusive. This is the most important and revolutionary concept of the One-Minute Scolding.

Parents, struggling to learn and apply this technique, deal with their own conflicting feelings and discover a new strength within themselves. This strength carries over to a variety of interpersonal relationships, not just the parent-child bond. The child learns with the parents how to express strong, even conflicting feelings honestly and appropriately.

For parents who are not accustomed to a healthy, appropriate discharge of anger, a thirty-second time limit seems insufficient. Too much unfinished anger is dammed up and ready to explode in an inappropriate way. So the One-Minute Scolding offers this parent both a safeguard in its time limit and a vehicle to express strong feelings appropriately. It also helps to terminate an issue that might otherwise have no clear ending.

The parent, as a mature adult, is strong enough to learn and undertake what may initially be uncomfortable. The ability to experience conflicting emotions while maintaining one's composure and sense of balance is the essence of maturity.

Difficult and unnatural as this close combination of opposite emotions strikes us, it is the identical pattern found in early attachment behaviors of infant and parent. It is the progression of feeling in both parent and child, of high excitation descending to relaxation, that produces bonding or attachment between the two. It is the One-Minute Scolding's ability to synthesize this pattern with the same sliding range of two strong feelings which accounts for its remarkable success as a disciplinary approach. By taking advantage of the high feeling states in the parents' reactions to misbehaviors and ending in a calm and comfortable state of relaxation, the One-Minute Scolding bonds parent to child and creates a closer attachment.

The underlying feeling patterns and their order and progression are the roots of the One-Minute Scolding's success. Like any good tool, the One-Minute Scolding has to be used properly for it to work well. Even though the scolding should never take more than a minute, it has to be administered with all of its parts and in the right order and manner. It shouldn't be used at all until the parent is clear about what to do and how to do it. A part of the scolding is worse than no scolding.

Although the One-Minute Scolding is simple in structure, it is sophisticated in nature. It is not necessary to understand its sophisticated nature in order to apply it or in order for it to work. It is necessary, however, to administer it correctly and consistently. In Chapter III we explain how the technique of the One-Minute Scolding was developed and improved over the last ten years, but you need not read that chapter in order to use the One-Minute Scolding yourself. Some parents, however, will appreciate the process of how we put together the scolding. For them, understanding its principles will encourage them in their efforts. Furthermore, they will see that its basic principles are applicable to many other interpersonal relationships.

Parents need support and encouragement in implementing the One-Minute Scolding technique at first. Old habits of discipline are not easy to change and when one tries to form a new habit it is easy to give up at the first hint of difficulty or resistance. Later in this book we address in detail the specific problems and difficulties that both parents and children encounter initially with this technique.

At this point, however, it is enough for you to know that administering the One-Minute Scolding is, in fact, easy. The difficulty comes in delivering the scolding consistently and maturely, even when it doesn't seem to be working right away. We can assure you that your hard work in sticking with this technique will be richly rewarded.

Some children whose problems are not severe learn quickly and respond within days with improved behavior and better feelings about themselves and their parents. Most children require a few weeks of consistent scolding before they respond positively. A few extremely difficult children require several months. But as long as you stay with the technique, you will eventually achieve your goal of improving your child's behavior while strengthening your own sense of joy and happiness within your family.

3

Love and the Best of Intentions Are Not Enough

The One-Minute Scolding was first conceived as a result of our efforts to help troubled adopted and foster children develop a bond or attachment to their parents. Because these children had all lost several sets of parents prior to their current placement, they had become unwilling or unable to trust that their new parents would not also abandon them. That intense, trusting relationship which is characteristic of the normal attachment between parent and child seemed to be an impossibility to them.

In search of some clues as to how we might break this impasse, we turned to the literature on bonding, the basic insight of which arises from an observation and analysis of parent/child interactions. Much useful information about bonding comes to us from animal behaviorists, such as Konrad Lorenz and Desmond Morris.

As almost everyone knows, baby mammals need milk to survive and only the mother can provide that milk. Should the mother forget her baby and wander off, the baby could die. Baby mammals are also relatively helpless and fall easy prey to predators if they are not protected by a parent. To guarantee the infant's survival, nature seems to have developed a set of behaviors for both infant and mother which causes an intense attachment to form between them. This bond compels the mother to return to her baby, to feed it, and to protect it. The bond also directs that baby mammal to stay close to its mother when hungry, frightened, or ill. That is why it is not recommended that humans get too close to a bear cub in the forest. The mother bear will soon arrive programmed to do all in her rather extensive power to save that baby.

Human infants require many years of protection and care if they are to survive and grow up, so the process of bonding between human parent and child is especially important. This bond does not come about automatically. We find many parents and children for whom this is a difficult process and a good, strong attachment has not been achieved. Sometimes the process has been interrupted by hospitalizations or other separations or losses of shorter or longer duration. Where the process has been fraught with the most severe difficulty, parents and children are conflicted and confused in their feelings towards each other. Almost invariably, those children develop serious problems and become deeply disturbed.

Empirically, then, we can readily verify the existence of an intense parent/child bond among most mammals and the destructive consequences of the absence of such a bond. Of critical importance, however, is the further question which behavioral scientists have not yet fully answered: How does this bond normally come into being, and how can it be developed in troubled older children who failed to form such an attachment at the usual time during infancy and childhood?

Let's look at a bonding process in action. For being such a small, helpless creature, a baby is capable of causing powerful feeling in its parents. When a baby, let us say, is wet and hungry, he can cry in a way that elicits a fairly prompt response. The response is prompt because that cry can cause the mother considerable tension and discomfort. By the time the baby's cry has reached a certain pitch, the mother will put aside her other concerns to hurry off and change the howling baby's diaper. She clucks and croons to him as she quickly cleans him up. Then she finds her comfortable chair, settles in with the child, and begins to feed or nurse him. Most of the time, both mother and child immediately begin to relax. The baby nestles into the curve of the mother's arm in a cozy and comfortable way. He sucks away happily and looks up at his mother. The mother looks back and they smile and coo to each other.

Studies by attachment theorist Bowlby and others have shown that maternal/infant attachment progresses extremely rapidly in the first few hours and days of an infant's life. In addition, they have found that touching, eye contact, crying, and physical interactions between the mother and the baby play vital roles in the development of this attachment. From these and other studies, as well as our observation of parents and children struggling to form satisfying attachments, we have concluded that it is those interactions between infant and parent (speaking, feeding, cooing, smiling, laughing, holding, touching) while going from a state of high excitation to a state of relaxation, which actually form the bond and then cause that bond to grow and to strengthen between the infant and the parent.

"Peek-a-boo" is a game mothers often play quite naturally with their babies. The game strengthens their bond.
It is also an excellent demonstration of bonding in action.

The mother hides her face behind her hands. The
baby cannot see her and responds with agitation and
then anxiety. "Mother has disappeared!" "Boo!" She
whips her hands away from her face. "Mama has returned!" The baby is flooded with relief and delight.
Over and over they repeat the game. It is an emotional
roller coaster for the baby: Mama is gone: Anxiety! Mama
returns: Delicious relief and joy! These games and variations of them are repeated day after day. Playfully, intuitively, the mother has created a ritual that strengthens their attachment. Such games prepare the child for
those real-life situations when the mother must be out
of sight for longer periods. The shortburst sessions of
peek-a-boo have taught the child that he might lose sight
of his mother for awhile and that, while this may cause
him anxiety, she will always return. In this way, the
child builds up trust.

Again, it is the process of high emotion in both the
mother and the child coming down to a relaxed state
that is the essence of bonding.

Because it is usually the mother who has the opportunity to play these bonding games and bring relief when

the child is distressed, the mother/child bond tends to be the strongest. However, this process works for anyone who has such an interaction with the child: father, grandparent, or sibling.

The leading exponent of attachment theory, John Bowlby, has emphasized that "there is a propensity in human beings to form strong, affectional bonds to significant others." He has explained that many forms of emotional distress and personality disorders in children are the consequence of separation and loss of a parent. The most intense emotions arise during the formation, maintenance, disruption, and renewal of attachment relationships. The threat of losing the parent arouses *anxiety* in the child, whereas actual loss gives rise to *sorrow*. Both the threat of loss and actual loss are likely to arouse *anger*.

Over an eighteen-month period we studied twenty-six children who had been taken from their natural parents because of neglect or abuse. Each had experienced

multiple placements in adoptive or foster homes by the time we saw them. Each was referred for psychiatric evaluation or treatment because of pervasive maladaptive behaviors and attitudes. We found that (1) none of the children had developed a satisfactory bond to their current parents; (2) some of them were able, even compelled, to evoke strong feelings from their new parents, but (3) they elicited these feelings by annoying or dangerous misbehavior which resulted in strong feelings, to be sure, but feelings which were also negative.

Their parents had all tried a variety of disciplinary measures and punishments to stop the negative behaviors in the children—spankings, rewards, restrictions—and though the punishments were frequently consistent and often harsh, they didn't get the more adaptive behaviors they had hoped for. Even though abandonment was what they feared most, these children risked behaving as though they expected—or even wanted—their parents to abandon them, just as the others before them had done.

Could it be that these children's antisocial and annoying behaviors, which constantly provoked high emotions in their parents, were some clumsy but elemental compulsion to initiate the first stage of bonding? If so, the adoptive parents were missing their cues. All of the parents revealed that eventually they resorted to one common form of response. In their annoyance and desperation, they banished the children from their proximity. "Go to your room!" or "I've had enough, I'm going out!" At the point of highly aroused feelings in both the parent and the child, the child was abandoned or distanced and the process was interrupted only to repeat itself like a needle stuck in a record. The children had achieved their feared goal: abandonment. When the family finally came for psychiatric help, the parents commonly admitted defeat and felt that someone else should take over the task of raising their difficult youngster. The parents felt angry and frustrated. Love and the best of intentions had not been enough, and there were no rewards. They felt like failures as parents. The children in turn sensed the imminent and feared response to their actions: another rejection and abandonment. Their actions were again self-defeating, their fears, self-fulfilling.

With the help of Bowlby's studies on attachment and bonding, we discovered a clue which resolved this vicious circle: children in danger or distress seek out and need the proximity of their parents to feel safe. Parents protect and are a source of gratification. While the child, in his own primitive manner, was seeking out all and any behavior necessary to arouse the intense feelings that launched or strengthened attachment, our parents were aborting the next step necessary: proximity. Unable to read the obscure meaning of the child's behavior, they were actually doing the opposite of what was necessary by banishing the youngster from their sight. Thus, a bond was not formed, and the attachment was not strengthened.

The bond itself became our "patient." Now the parents had to be taught to continue the bonding process to the end in order to facilitate attachment. We instructed the parents not to punish their children with banishment or withdrawal. Instead, they were told that when the child misbehaved to take the child on their laps, and to scold him or her vigorously and with feeling. By the time the child had been aroused to an emotional response (sad look, tear, a bowed head), both parent and child would be in a state of strong feeling. The parents then were to change their tone abruptly and become warm and loving.

They were to reassure the child of the permanence of their relationship and to tell the child of their real care and concern for him.

In this ritualized "bonding exercise," we taught the parents to be intensely negative and intensely positive in the interaction, because the wall of defenses that the child had learned to hide behind needed to be penetrated. The defensive wall "kept the parents out" so that the child could remain untouched. This the parent had to conquer with the expression of strong feeling.

Because of the parent's propensity to prolong the scolding, a time limit was set so that the parent would change abruptly from intense negative feeling (lasting no longer than thirty seconds) to intense positive feeling (also thirty seconds) before the child had time to rebuild his defensive walls. This way he would still be open to warmth and love.

At first, the parents found it hard to believe that this simple exercise was going to change their child's behavior. Their dramatic punishments had gotten them nowhere, to be sure. But a reinterpretation of the children's behavior as a clumsy gesture of attachment needs began to make sense to them.

With strong support from a parents' group and their therapists, all of the parents made brave efforts at home. To their surprise, significant changes in their children became apparent almost right away. Although there were failures and regressions, we discovered that, whenever parents were able to use the One-Minute Scolding consistently, not only did children misbehave less, but the feeling/tone of the parent-child relationship improved dramatically as well. Where once the child's neediness was manifested by clinging, whining, and attention-seeking behaviors, the parents now reported the child to be more direct, affectionate, and playful. Slowly, one could see the development of conscience. Care and consideration began to replace the atmosphere of warring camps.

As we began teaching more parents and other professionals interested in using our technique, we looked for additional theoretical understanding to improve and define the effectiveness of this new bonding strategy. We also wanted to understand better just why the One-Minute Scolding was an effective discipline in changing behavior. There are several important elements which aided the technique.

CONSISTENCY AND REPETITION

Important elements in learning are consistency and repetition. Parents who became consistent in their response to a child's misbehavior were rewarded by the child's ability to learn new and more appropriate behaviors. Children learn unevenly and sometimes seem to resist the teaching process. Effective teachers and parents seem to understand that propensity in children and they know that children do not learn a lesson once and for all. They anticipate forgetfulness and even though it may be boring or irksome at times, they are consistent and they repeat the right answer or the correct behavior over and over again.

THE RIGHT STRENGTH OF FEELING

It is important that the forcefulness of the parent not be exaggerated because the child will then shift his attention to the parent and away from the lesson. Children are afraid of rageful parents, particularly a rageful father. Fear tends to preoccupy them with their need for safety and it becomes impossible for them to attend to the lesson.

PRIVACY AND DISTRACTION

If a laughing or teasing sibling stands on the sidelines, that too will distract the child. The scolding is best given in privacy where one can have the child's undivided attention. One might see the One-Minute Scolding as a process within which the child's attention is focused on a lesson to be learned.

CLARITY

With the right degree of feeling and in a nondistracting environment, the lesson must now be delivered with utmost clarity. Distinctly and repeatedly the child is given the lesson: "We don't hit people in this house. I don't want you to hit your sister. Hitting is ugly behavior and I get very angry with you when you hit your sister."

THE RIGHT LENGTH OF TIME

A parent cannot drone on and on with the lesson because children learn to "tune out." Once the child is no longer paying attention to the parent, learning stops. The child's attention has drifted off and the message is unheard. A "tuned out" parent also loses interest in teaching.

REWARD

Children learn best when they are rewarded for desired behavior. First, the children listen to the lesson and then we reward them for listening. The abrupt switch from a high-intensity scolding tone to a tone of assurance and affection brings a pleasant relief for the child, but it is also rather confusing and disorienting. It feels as though his emotional and psychological set must make an about-face; now he must focus in an entirely new and different direction. The affectionate words carry the message to him again and the child hears the "lesson" even more clearly.

> "You know, I think you're such a nifty and special fellow. When you play happily with your sister and when you're having a good time, it makes me happy. I like being your Mama and I want to be the very best Mama possible. No matter how naughty you are sometimes, I'll never leave you. Instead, I'll help you. Every time you hit, I'll scold you until you can remember that hitting is not allowed. I'll do that because I love you so much."

The child likes his parents to talk to him in this way. That warm approval of who he is, that assurance of love, rewards him for listening and paying attention to the lesson presented in the first half of the scolding. It feels good to be praised and treated like this.

THE OTHER SIDE OF THE DEFENSE BARRIER

The abrupt transition from being angry and upset to being warm and reassuring is a particularly important facet of the One-Minute Scolding. Parents may find that it feels somewhat uncomfortable or contrived at first, especially if they have a large backlog of undischarged anger left over from other frustrations. They may find the balance difficult to create between anger and love. They have to be convinced themselves that anger does not cancel out love. But practice and the formula of the One-Minute Scolding itself will help the parent strike a more natural balance in time.

It is for the well-defended child that this abrupt switch of affect is particularly important. Such a child has learned to keep his parents "out," to refuse to let his parents' feelings and actions touch him in any significant way. Children who develop this defense to an extreme are likely to develop sociopathic ways of dealing with life's problems. These are the children who have difficulty developing a conscience that works. The abrupt change of affect from anger to love in the One-Minute Scolding is an effective way for parents to catch such a defensive youngster off guard and touch him suddenly with positive feelings. This reverses the development of a defensive and antisocial lifestyle.

The use of the One-Minute Scolding gives the parents a framework within which to deal with their own feelings appropriately. An explosive, destructive father or a nagging, complaining mother can be transformed into a parent who expresses feelings about their child's behavior in a mature and adaptive way. The father doesn't hurl the rollerskate against the garage door but rather, states clearly, "I get mad as heck when I find your toys scattered all over the driveway where they rust, get lost, or cause accidents." He incorporates his feeling expression into the scolding. In so doing, not only is he able to discharge his anger immediately and safely, but he is also able to continue to teach the lesson he wants the child to learn. When a parent uses a mature expression of angry feeling, the child, in turn, learns not only that (1) feeling anger and expressing how you feel is natural and right, but also that (2) there is an appropriate and adaptive way to express those feelings. "If my Dad is angry at me, he tells me. This does not mean that he doesn't love me anymore."

A mature and adaptive way to express anger does *not* do the following:

- *Blame:* "You make me mad!" Rather: "I get awfully mad when . . .";
- *Act out:* such as hurling the rollerskate against the garage door and cursing;
- *Humiliate the other person:* "You rotten, sniveling kid!"; or, finally,
- *Muddy the issue directly at hand:* "You let the garbage pile up again, and, last week, you just left the garden tools outside, and . . ." Rather: "Each evening after supper, I want you to take out the garbage."

To be angry is natural and its immediate expression does not have to destroy anyone or anything. Neither does anger mean: "I don't love you anymore."

Many families now use this technique and we have found that if the parents are able to use it consistently and in the prescribed way, it can replace or augment most other forms of discipline. Some parents find that "time out" or "natural consequences" can give spice and variety to a parent's discipline. Most disciplinary measures can be effective if administered in a kind, firm, and consistent way. It is that form of discipline, however, that sends the child away or leaves either the child or the parent still very upset, that is neither wise nor positively effective.

After ten years of using the One-Minute Scolding we have seen the following effects:

- It changes the child's behavior, teaching him to choose those behaviors that reward him with a satisfying state of affairs for himself and for those around him.
- It teaches the child that his behaviors have consequences.
- It teaches the value of working through a problem in communication.
- It gives both parent and child a framework and model for the adaptive expression of feelings.
- It forms and/or strengthens the bond between parent and child, and it teaches trust.
- In teaching trust, it enables the child to develop a conscience, to which trust is the necessary first step.
- It is a technique that is useful for any family with children.

4 | What Is Good Discipline?

Good behavior is learned. It does not come about naturally. Children learn how to behave primarily from their parents but also from brothers, sisters, relatives, friends, neighbors, and teachers. Discipline means to teach and it is the chief means by which parents can help their children learn good behavior. Hence, it is important to identify those qualities which make one variety of discipline better than another. That is, what is good discipline?

Good discipline is:

- Immediate
- Consistent
- Certain
- Easily applied
- Fair
- Positive
- Appropriate in intensity
- Effective

Good discipline does not:
- Leave unfinished business or loose ends
- Change the rules in the middle of the game

- Indulge in hollow threats and idle warnings
- Have to be severe
- Require heroic efforts to be effective
- Humiliate
- Hurt relationships
- Leave parent and/or child feeling bad about themselves

GOOD DISCIPLINE IS IMMEDIATE

When a child knows he has broken the rule he should, and usually does, feel guilty. But "feeling guilty" is useful only when it will help the offender change his ways as soon as possible. So the youngster need not be overwhelmed by guilt, nor should he spend a long time worrying about possible consequences. Prolonged anxiety serves no useful purpose. As soon as a parent is aware that her child has made a mistake, she must take it up with her child and discipline her. The child must learn that wrong or dangerous behaviors have consequences, at least the consequence of a scolding. The mistake and the discipline must be strongly linked together.

GOOD DISCIPLINE IS CONSISTENT

When parents ignore some mistakes and descend like avenging angels at other times, children become confused. If a toddler toys with the television controls and meets with approval or indifference on some occasions and is severely scolded on others, she is unsure of what she should do with those enticing dials.

It is equally confusing when one parent punishes a child for behavior that the other parent ignores or even encourages. Such inconsistencies teach the child that neither the parents nor their rules are to be trusted. Being consistent gives order and security to a child whose world looks chaotic and frightening at times. A predictable response allows the youngster the freedom to get on with life so she does not have to expend all of her energies exploring the extent of her boundaries and testing the sincerity of her parents.

To be consistent as a parent is not easy. It implies a commitment to the child and a maturity about the responsibilities of raising him. It also takes energy. Mothers and fathers must agree on rules and help each other to be consistent. Divorced parents will want to agree over issues that concern their children. Numerous picky rules are too hard to enforce consistently. So, it is wise to agree on rules that are vital and valuable, clear and age-appropriate. A lapse in consistency does not mean failure. Look for support. Try again.

GOOD DISCIPLINE IS CERTAIN

Children are not impressed by idle threats and hollow warnings. They know exactly by the tone of your voice if you mean what you just said. Children will often break a rule if experience suggests there is ambivalence about this rule. In large part, the effectiveness of discipline is determined by its certainty and not its severity.

When children know beyond a shadow of a doubt that you mean what you say, they can internalize that voice and behave even when you are not there to check on them.

GOOD DISCIPLINE IS EASILY APPLIED
ALMOST ANYWHERE

We have already noted that if it is to be effective, discipline must be immediate, consistent, and absolutely certain. In turn, this means that any effective disciplinary strategy must also be reasonably easy to apply and be applicable most anywhere. For if it is not, the disciplinary strategy will, in fact, be uniquely ineffective in that it simply will not be used at all. Being immediate, consistent, and certain in discipline is hard even for the best of parents, so good discipline had better be easy to apply under almost any conditions.

GOOD DISCIPLINE IS FAIR

Very early in life, children develop an intense sense of justice. Most children know when they have made a mistake, and they tend to expect to be disciplined for that mistake. Though the response may range from a mild reproach to a thundering scolding, the child needs to understand that he made a mistake and that discipline is a logical consequence of this faulty choice.

But some matters and rules are more important than others. Let's say a child accidentally spills a glass of milk across the dinner table and receives a harsh tongue-lashing, "Clumsy oaf! Every night we go through this . . ." After all, a personal sense of worthiness is far more valuable than a wet tablecloth. The child will feel unfairly treated and diminished. However, if he is skateboarding down a busy street and is nearly hit by a car, his own sense of fairness will lead him to feel that stern discipline is in order and certainly fair.

Children who are disciplined unfairly do not learn from that discipline, but concentrate on their feelings of being treated unfairly. This defeats the purpose of the discipline, which is to teach good behavior.

GOOD DISCIPLINE IS POSITIVE

Nobody needs the lessons learned from negative discipline. The parent who humiliates his child or condemns the child rather than the deed does real damage. If, whenever she makes a mistake, little Nancy is told by her mother that she is a bad girl and someone who never does anything right, Nancy will, in time, come to believe that her mother is right. She will learn that lesson well. Her self-image will plummet, and her mother's angry words will become a self-fulfilling prophecy. She will become everything her mother called her. Simultaneously, her mother will feel unhappy and inept about her abilities as a parent.

Good discipline is positive. It offers help, a solution, and the promise of continued help. It does not leave the child without a solution. It does not diminish his person. It teaches good behavior in a way that rewards and reinforces the attachment between parent and child and leaves both feeling basically good about themselves and the other.

GOOD DISCIPLINE IS APPROPRIATE
IN INTENSITY

Decent table manners are generally conceded to be desirable accomplishments. Yet few parents would seriously attempt to classify them as matters of life and death. A mother who "goes into orbit" when her Justin drops the juice pitcher will not be taken seriously by anybody, nor does she deserve to be. Her son is not likely to have fewer accidents as a result of the rantings.

The inappropriate and excessive intensity of the mother's response has both discredited her in the eyes of her child and resulted in "overload" in the child's learning system. Imagine the decibel this mother will have to reach when she reacts to Justin's tailgating experiments with his bicycle on the busy road! Tailgating (hanging onto a moving car to pick up a little speed) is a life-threatening situation, and it would be appropriate to respond by "pulling out all the stops." We would want a child to learn this lesson once and for all because there may not be a second chance. An extremely intense response, presuming that it does not lapse into hysteria, is entirely appropriate for this mistake. So we save our "big guns" for the big issues and modulate our response so that our reaction is appropriate to the "crime."

Furthermore, intensity must be tailor-made to the degree of sensitivity of the child. Some children are very sensitive and don't require such highly charged responses. Others need an extra dose of intensity in order to be reached at all.

GOOD DISCIPLINE IS EFFECTIVE

Remember, to discipline means to teach. This is the "bottom line," the ultimate criterion of good discipline: Does this or that disciplinary strategy actually teach good behavior?

Now let's see if the One-Minute Scolding qualifies as a good disciplinary technique by examining it in the light of the criteria we have just identified.

THE ONE-MINUTE SCOLDING IS IMMEDIATE

The One-Minute Scolding can and should be used as soon as the parent has recognized that the child has misbehaved or broken a rule. There is no need to wait, because the One-Minute Scolding can take place anywhere and at any time. In ordinary circumstances, the child should be taken off privately so that the intense parent/child interaction, which is essential if the desired learning is to take place, will not be diluted or the child distracted by the presence of onlookers or other interesting stimuli. However, there are times and circumstances when total privacy is not possible and scolding in front of others is entirely appropriate. For instance, if a parent is driving on a freeway and her children continue to misbehave in the back seat despite several warnings, she drives off at the next exit, parks the car safely and takes each offending child out of the car and scolds him intensely in full view of the other occupants.

Children will tend to obey Mom the next time she warns them in a similar circumstance.

THE ONE-MINUTE SCOLDING IS CONSISTENT

Being consistent is extremely important in any system of discipline. Yet, for most parents, consistency is an elusive goal indeed. The One-Minute Scolding has a ready-to-use and quick formula which encourages parental consistency. It is easy to learn, reasonable, and will not induce unnecessary guilt. Hence, most of the "roadblocks" that prevent parents from being consistent have been removed. It still requires a mature and responsible parent to consistently discipline a child, but herein lies the real success of this discipline. The more you persevere, the sooner you will reap the rewards of your efforts.

THE ONE-MINUTE SCOLDING IS CERTAIN

In this formula there is no room for hollow threat or idle warning. Dad clearly states that Nelly is to return promptly from the movies. A time has been set and there is no ambivalence. If she is late she will be scolded and the "threat" of a scolding each time she is late is no hollow threat. Her dad loves her. So he makes both the rule clear and the scolding certain.

THE ONE-MINUTE SCOLDING IS EASILY APPLIED ALMOST ANYWHERE

The One-Minute Scolding can be extremely effective when whispered fiercely in the ear of a small child who refuses to behave in the supermarket and gently finished with a hug. Observers will silently, or perhaps not so silently, applaud that parent who has the courage and conviction to discipline a child in a public place. The child will learn that certain behaviors are not appropriate in supermarkets, restaurants, and other public places. Others being present will not be a protection from getting a scolding. The One-Minute Scolding can be used wherever it is needed.

THE ONE-MINUTE SCOLDING IS FAIR

Children do not like the One-Minute Scolding, but they admit that it is basically fair. They know that it is the consequence of the bad behavior. They know they have made a mistake. They *expect* to be disciplined. They expect to be taught not to repeat that misbehavior. The timing and formula itself prevent unfair draggings on, or any additional restrictions.

THE ONE-MINUTE SCOLDING IS POSITIVE

The child is scolded for her misdeed. This is clearly stated. The child has made a mistake. The child is neither condemned nor put down for making a mistake. Rather, the child is told that the parent is angry, upset, or annoyed because the child chose to make that mistake. The child herself is never treated negatively—only her negative behavior is.

Furthermore, the second half of the One-Minute Scolding allows the parent a good opportunity to be positive about her child and about their relationship.

"I love you. I think you are a fine person. You are a fine girl. You made a mistake, but I understand. You are going to learn how not to make that mistake and to choose the right behavior because I am going to help you. Every time you make a mistake, I'll remind you with a scolding. That's because I love you so much. That's why I discipline you and I scold you." This is one of the most important aspects of the One-Minute Scolding, because it provides a place for the loving affirmation of the child's person directly following an angry response to a misdeed. Personhood and behaviors do not cancel each other out. Anger and love do not negate each other.

THE ONE-MINUTE SCOLDING IS APPROPRIATE IN INTENSITY

The intensity of the scolding and of the warm and caring feelings expressed in the second half of the scolding can be varied in intensity by the parent's good judgment. As parents become comfortable and at ease in using the One-Minute Scolding, they sharpen their ability to choose the intensity appropriate to the size of the misdeed as well as to the sensitivity of the child.

Very sensitive children (easily moved to tears with a mild scolding) need very much less intensity, or they remain anxious and fearful, always ready to flee from an angry parent.

Temperamentally hard-to-reach children, who have already developed a wall that does not admit feelings need an intensity that is very strong. The first half of the scolding where anger and frustration are expressed must be strong and penetrating. The second half of the scolding must be equally intense! Rib-cracking hugs, cheeks pinched, a tuft of hair tugged—it takes that kind of physical intensity to penetrate the defensiveness of some children because they would otherwise miss the feelings of intense affection they need to feel from you.

Even when it does not come naturally, temperamentally soft, gentle, "laid-back," or overly relaxed parents have to learn how to relate with this kind of intensity.

THE ONE-MINUTE SCOLDING IS EFFECTIVE

After teaching the One-Minute Scolding for ten years to parents, teachers, and to other family therapists, we have seen it to be a remarkably effective discipline. It teaches the child to expect uncomfortable consequences both of mistakes in judgment and in the breaking of family rules. It teaches how one deals with anger. It rewards the child for listening to the parent's explanation of what the mistake was and of the feelings it has caused in the parent. It clearly teaches the child what behavior is good and what behavior is not acceptable. It teaches the child that the parent cares for him and wants to be a responsible, loving parent.

In our experience, when parents have used the One-Minute Scolding consistently and in the prescribed way, in nearly all cases, a marked improvement has occurred in the behavior of the children very soon after the initiation of the method.

Just as there are children who experience difficulty learning arithmetic and who need special help, so also there are children who have difficulty learning how to behave and who require a longer time span of consistent, frequent, and intense discipline—weeks or months. And there are those few who unfortunately require individual therapy and special programs that go beyond the capabilities of parentally administered One-Minute Scoldings.

5

All He Needs Is a Good Spanking

Punishment is not an effective discipline. Furthermore, it interferes with the trusting relationship that the parent and child must form. Punishment and discipline are not the same thing. Discipline means to teach. But punishment, as the dictionary points out, "is to subject a person to pain, loss, confinement, death, etc. as a *penalty* for some offense, transgression or fault."

Children make many mistakes in their choices and behaviors, so they need to be guided and helped. They need to be taught appropriate behavior. They *do* need discipline. They do not need punishment, because punishments usually cause more harm than help.

Almost any punishment can snuff out an undesirable behavior if you scare the youngster enough, or hurt him, or use force. The result is quick but the effect is often short-lived. Only the side effects of punishment become well-entrenched in the child's personality.

Punishment in its many forms is no stranger to any of us. It is still the more familiar experience in our personal past and in history. Punishment is one of the oldest forms of social control known to humankind. Early educational guides in child rearing encouraged the use of punishment in ample doses. The schoolmaster used a dunce cap and a stick to "teach" his lessons. "Spare the rod and spoil the child," an isolated Biblical statement, is often the only Biblical instruction some parents manage to remember. Adults themselves are not exempt from punishment. We are reprimanded for inappropriate actions or mistakes or penalized for breaking the law. We receive traffic tickets, have our licenses taken away, and may be sent to jail for certain infractions. Over the years psychiatrists, psychologists, educators, and other students of child development and human behavior have examined the effects of punishment on the individual. Those who dared question the long-range effectiveness of punishment were often misunderstood. Where fear and force were reduced or removed as goads to good behavior and where the value of better behavior was not yet learned and internalized, confusion reigned and problems brewed. Small wonder that many returned to punishment in a panic to restore order. But students of human behavior continued to examine the effects of punishment on the individual and though they followed different roads, they arrived at conclusions that were remarkably similar and are now generally accepted as fact.

Punishment can alter behavior, but the change that may be immediate is also usually temporary and short-lived. If Olaf pinches his provocative little brother and his mama spanks him for it and locks him in his room, he will not pinch his brother again, at least not while he is locked in his room. But he will probably pinch his little brother another time when the provocation arises. Or he will change his attack and slap him, since it was pinching that was punished and, after all, mama slaps. Olaf learns to be sneaky and clever, not kind.

The driver ticketed for speeding will usually resume his old behavior within a few days, but exerting greater vigilance for hidden speed traps. He has learned cunning, not safe driving. These changes in behavior tend to be temporary precisely because the individuals have not learned and incorporated the values in question, but simply react to external force or pressure.

Once the threat of punishment is removed, the "bad" behavior often returns full strength. One has simply learned how to avoid punishment by misbehaving when the authority is not around. This points out that force and fear do not direct one towards learning the values of wiser, safer, more appropriate behaviors. The lesson and its value are not learned—and neither is the better behavior.

Many of us have experienced moments when we have punished or have been tempted to punish. We wish to use some harsh or violent treatment to "nip this action in the bud"—to "stop this behavior once and for all." We react with a punishment because we have allowed our own feelings of fear or impatience to flood us and overwhelm us. But if we have made a habit of such seemingly short-cut techniques and we wish to make some basic changes to improve our relationships with our children, we must learn to translate our punishments into discipline, and we shall have to consider the long-term side effects of common punishments.

Punishments may stop a given misbehavior quickly (perhaps even permanently), but the consequences may cause a variety of seriously destructive side effects. The side effects may induce a whole new range of misbehaviors—as in lying, stealing, cheating, shoplifting, or fire-setting. Or the side effects of harsh and unreasonable punishments may cause "internal injuries"—psychic scars or wounds that impair happy, healthy functioning. These include inhibitions, intense anxiety, phobias, night fears, bedwetting, low self-esteem, neurotic guilt, fear of risk, anger turned inwards or anger or aggression turned toward all others. Punishment destroys child/parent relationships. It scars the psyche, fosters the sneak, and generates the bully.

Spanking is most commonly used in extreme situations, such as when a child runs into traffic or plays with fire. Spanking, happily, is being used less and less in families today, as parents and professionals realize that such physical punishments are painful, embarrassing and fear-inducing experiences. Spanking in its variations—slapping, hitting, belting, beating—is rarely effective if not dangerous. In the child, it produces more a memory and resentment for the humiliation, pain, and fear inflicted in him, than a clear memory of the lesson he was meant to learn. The parents who spank feel guilt that physical punishment has only estranged them from their child. They realize that as parents they have only discharged and relieved their own anger and fear through such punishment. Parents do not like to hurt their children and they don't like to see that they have left their youngster sullen, devious, and rebellious as a result. Children who are physically punished learn that physical violence is a way to express frustration, fear, and disappointment. They learn to hit and bully others rather than to behave properly and learn the value of another person. That alone makes spanking a harmful, ineffective, and self-perpetuating punishment.

Withholding food, a previously earned reward, an allowance, or affection is another common punishment for misbehavior. Food is a powerful symbol of parental care and affection. When parents withhold meals, deny desserts or even use foods as bribes, they start up a whole tangle of eating and drinking problems for a child that can complicate his life well into his adulthood.

> Willy gives his sister a swift kick under the table because she is "tattling" on him. With this double infraction he is sent from the table by his exasperated mother. "No dessert," she says. So Willy scuffs off to his room, feeling angry and mistreated. Later when his mother tries to re-establish a friendly relationship with him by offering him his chocolate pudding Willy refuses it with feigned disinterest to pay his mother back. Now his mom feels rejected and hurt. If Willy doesn't like her dessert, Willy doesn't like her. So she, too, withdraws into wounded silence.

Willy has not learned to express his anger appropriately. His sister hasn't learned that tattling is wrong. His mother resorts to withholding sweets as a ticket to reaching him. Everyone is estranged and feeling bad because Willy was punished rather than disciplined.

Banishment is commonly used as a punishment today. Parents are often encouraged to send their children to their bedrooms for "time out," or to "think about it" when they misbehave.

> Erica has been told by her papa to clear the dinner dishes. With righteous indignation she states that this is an unfair request. It is her sister Elena's turn. Erica did the dishes last night, so she refused to obey her father's orders. Her father is angry with Erica's disobedience and orders her to her room until she has decided to be obedient. Erica marches out of the kitchen and up to her room, furious and determined not to give in to this unfair treatment. Erica cannot survive in her room for the rest of her days being angry and thinking ugly thoughts—so only more

unfairness is her lot. She has to "give in" to her father. Or, perhaps, her father has to "give in" to her?

We would say that their relationship is strained. One or the other of them could "give in" out of maturity. The father could relieve the situation by going to Erica and kindly offering to discuss their differences and resolve their problem. It would have been easier if the father had protected their relationship by disciplining Erica first for her disobedience and then dealing with Erica's feelings about being unfairly treated.

Isolation or banishment of a child is an insidious and sometimes even malevolent form of punishment. Left alone with a wide range of feelings, rage, feelings of retaliation and revenge as well as worry, guilt, and shame, a child feels abandoned and not at all certain there is anything left worth redeeming in themselves. When children misbehave they deserve the right to know that there are solutions to their behavior problems. They must know that they will not be abandoned or rejected or that their mistakes make them intrinsically bad or unworthy of love and help. They deserve to know that parents are a source of safety and solutions and that they will offer comfort and security when things are in disarray. Stuffed animals and pets in a lonely bedroom cannot help them solve the situation.

Humiliation and hostile attacks destroy a child's self-confidence and self-esteem with devastating certainty. Ridicule and humiliation are sometimes used by parents as a form of punishment.

Carla drops a dish she is wiping and it breaks. Her father, preoccupied and irritated by problems at work, barks at her. He calls her a "fumbling, clumsy klutz" and instructs her to clean up "her mess" and "be more careful next time." Carla is a normal sensitive girl. Breaking the dish was an accident and not a malicious act. Her father's words feel cruel and defining. They only prove to her that she is clumsy. Why, she stumbled over Victor's feet in school yesterday. Yes, she must be a clumsy klutz. She feels dreadfully embarrassed and bad about who she is. She certainly does not think about wiping the dishes more carefully.

Repeated humiliations and serious ridicule will erode a child's self-esteem to the point where she will have few or no friends, she will do poorly in school, and will be convinced that she is somehow a defective or bad person. She will lose interest in how she dresses or takes care of her things. She will feel defeated, give up easily, and put herself down at the slightest provocation.

Defining a person with negative traits will only teach her to become what you define her to be. Parents don't like seeing their children reduced to such a fate. They enjoy watching a child grow to feeling good about themselves and about who they are.

There are other parental tactics or responses to misbehaviors which, although not punishments, are not helpful in teaching children how to behave. *Threats* leave a child wondering which ones will come true and which ones won't. As threats are easier to state than to follow up, the child soon learns to dismiss them and you as full of hot air, and dismiss the parent as not being sincere. Creating overblown possible consequences to minor crimes only operates on the principle of fear and offers the child no alternative way of behaving.

Ignoring behaviors is the parents' way of avoiding issues that need serious attention consistently. Ambivalence in the parents' minds may be the cause of just "not noticing" what is going on. Misbehavior has to be taken seriously if you love your youngster. On the other hand, neither is one required to be on the child's back about every little thing.

Work as punishment spoils the beauty and joy one can receive from doing a job well or from cooperating with others while doing a chore. To be sent back to pick up after oneself is certainly a reasonable consequence when a job is left unfinished. But to heap more work on what was already difficult to accomplish, compounds the issue and offers no help.

Restrictions are easy to pronounce in a fit of frustration and are hard to enforce later on, so they usually break down early. "Two weeks of being grounded" or a "month of no TV" is usually a greater punishment for the parent to enforce than it is for the child to endure. Anger hangs in the air over both parties for too long and the child often knows that the parent will give in eventually.

Loss of privileges, like restrictions, are easier to invent than to enforce. To make a point about a bicycle left in the rain once too often, putting it up for a short time may underline how serious you are about the issue. But it is important not to overdo the length of time you take the privilege away or else the child will remember the incident only as an injustice and not as the lesson you meant for him to learn.

Consequences to be faced squarely as the result of a mistake or lack in judgment are a good teacher to us all and certainly remain a part of all experience. A child should not be protected from every unpleasant consequence he incurs. But as the only disciplinary tactic, waiting for the consequences of a behavior is not always practical. The consequence of not finding your bed in a messy bedroom could take a few weeks. On the other hand, the consequences of riding a skateboard in heavy traffic may never produce another opportunity from which to learn again.

The ultimate criterion for judging a disciplinary tactic is simple: Does it teach good behavior? As outlined in the preceding pages, although it's clear that punishment may temporarily or intermittently prevent bad behavior, it does not teach good behavior, and it does not internalize the parental voice as conscience.

While defective in these primary purposes, punishment is remarkably effective and reliable in producing the following secondary effects:

- It destroys parent/child relationships.
- It fosters the sneak and generates the bully.
- It causes anxiety and rage in the punished child and often in the punishing parent.
- It causes anxiety which actually interferes with the learning of the desired new behavior.

From their own experience, most parents learn instinctively what the behavioral scientists have discovered experimentally. Punishment does not teach good behavior effectively and has many destructive side effects.

To discipline is *not* to punish *because* to punish is *not* to teach.

6 How Conscience Develops

Conscience is an important goal of all of our efforts at discipline. Far more important than reestablishing peace and quiet, or temporarily stopping offensive behavior, is the teaching of healthy behaviors and the values that underlie them. Parents hope that when their children are left unsupervised, or have left home for the last time, they will ultimately become independent, and that they will be functioning as happy and honorable members of a family and a community. In other words, parents hope that their children will have a *conscience*, which includes both a sense of what is right and the will and conviction to follow it.

What is this conscience that parents want for their children? Most experts of human behavior would agree that it includes the following:

- The ability to behave honestly and to withstand temptation towards antisocial behavior.
- The ability to defer immediate gratification for more distant rewards.

- The ability to feel anxiety when considering misbehavior.
- The ability to feel guilt or remorse after misbehaving.

This combination of behaviors and feelings gives the individual the tools with which to behave appropriately and comfortably in society.

The idea of conscience is neither old-fashioned nor outdated, despite the inclination of some to relegate it to the quaint environs of the Sunday School classroom. Quite the contrary, a developed conscience is essential to the health of both the individual and society. Its absence is manifest in the all-too-familiar symptoms of crime and violence. Children, adolescents, and adults with well-formed consciences rarely commit crimes.

Conscience does not just happen. It is taught to the child, directly and indirectly, by his parents and other significant persons primarily in the first six or seven years of his life. The essential, nondispensable precondition for this teaching process which we call conscience formation is a relationship of trust between child and teaching adult. A glance at the normal developmental sequence of a child makes the reason for this readily understandable.

Normally, as the child grows, he associates security, warmth, and caring with his parents. They feed, nurture, and protect him. Although they are often a source of frustration to the child, they are primarily felt as consistent and loving beings. Hence, without any significant need to erect barriers with which to protect himself from his parents, the child becomes one with the parents and takes in their warmth and values as shared by word and example.

If, on the other hand, the relationship is troubled and

conflicted, the intended message of warmth, caring, and firmness may not be sent by the parent and/or received by the child. As a result, the child does not become one with the parent and does not take in the parent's values. Conscience formation does not occur.

There are many factors which may negatively affect both conscience formation and the trusting relationship between parent and child which must precede and accompany conscience development. Most of these factors can be grouped into three major categories:

- Parental problems.
- Temperament of the child.
- Fate.

PARENTAL PROBLEMS

Parents may be ineffective in forming a trusting relationship with their child for many reasons. One recent study (Glueck) followed potential delinquents from the age of two or three through the late adolescent years and found that two parental factors highly correlated with delinquency and poor conscience-formation. Parents with serious emotional problems, such as schizophrenia and alcoholism, or with a history of delinquency themselves, have a high percentage of children with delinquency. Preoccupied with their own emotional and psychological problems, they fail to direct consistent efforts toward developing a close, trusting relationship with their child. The child may well be seeking and be fully open to such a relationship and to a parent who will teach him values and proper behaviors, but if the parent's attention is focused elsewhere, or nowhere, conscience formation will not occur.

For the same reason, parents with troubled marriages have difficulty creating the warm, secure family environment that is the precondition for the transmission of values to their children. Their energies are diverted from child care and instruction to coping with problems in the marriage relationship. The same may be said of parents struggling with work, physical health, and alcohol problems.

Another common, but poorly understood, factor that seems to interfere with conscience formation arises from the parent teaching the child to turn to himself when in trouble or need. For whatever reason, be it parental disinterest, incompetence, or ideology, the child is taught to seek his own solutions to moral issues and to expect neither parental nor societal guidance for certain choices. He learns to choose behaviors on a pragmatic basis rather than because he fears the consequences of bad behavior—namely guilt and remorse. Whenever he turns to his parents or to others for guidance and instruction, he receives their smiling confidence that he can handle the problem alone. Inevitably, he comes to perceive his parents as distant and even weak, and he fears that they may not be strong enough to help him with his fears and difficulties. Frustrated in his need for guidance and instruction, he is at the same time afraid to express his fear and rage because to do so may drive these weak parents even further away. Feeling essentially alone and unprotected in a frightening world, he sets out to create a "safe place" for himself by controlling and manipulating every aspect of his environment, including his parents. He becomes "the observer," and not a participant, not the one responsible for making his own choices and mistakes.

Aided only by his expanding ability to manipulate and control his environment, the child is compelled to use every bit of his psychic energy and skill to prevent further abandonment by his parents. He recognizes that his intense feelings of fear and rage might reduce the effectiveness of his perpetual vigilance and thus interfere with his ability to control and manipulate the environment. So he learns to "numb out" these and most other feelings. In time, this child is rendered unteachable. He is distant and emotionally unavailable to his parents. Hence, any ethical formation that occurs in him is strictly intellectual and thus fragile and susceptible to collapse under even moderate pressure. It lacks the deep, affective/experiential grounding necessary to support moral values under pressure. Thus, even modest temptation may be sufficient to radically alter his moral position on any given issue. In any case, his sole preoccupation is survival: he must control and manipulate his environment in any fashion necessary to guarantee that nothing can cause him injury or harm.

Even when parents are clear and consistent about their own values, they may not be aware of their child's need for explicit direction. For example, when Alphonse is angry with his sister, he hits her. Although his parents may hold it as a value that children work out their own problems, they need to teach Alphonse that there are more appropriate ways to express his feelings.

Parents with unconscious conflicts about obeying authority may subtly encourage their child to disobey laws. While paying lip service to the prevailing authority, they may smile quietly and give emotional support to their child when he chooses to disobey. The child is sent conflicting messages about the proper way to respond to a rule: overtly, he is taught to obey the law, but covertly, through the power of his parents' repressed feelings, he is told to disobey.

An unusually malignant injury is inflicted when one parent unconsciously encourages a child to disobey the family rules in order to antagonize or hurt the other parent. For example, a father may unconsciously reward some of his daughter's behaviors which are particularly upsetting to her mother. If this pattern persists, the child will tend to disdain her parents and scorn their rules as a means of coping with life's problems.

Some parents insist on very high standards for their children's behavior, and then not only do they fail to discipline them for their mistakes, but they actually reward them for their misbehaviors by showing excited interest in what their children have just done. This significantly interferes with conscience formation and, worse still, seems to elicit defiant and antisocial behavior from the child. For example, a mother harangues her fifteen-year-old daughter, Julia, forbidding her to date an eighteen-year-old boyfriend. Yet when Julia defies her mother and comes home from an outing with the forbidden boyfriend, not only does the mother not discipline her, but instead displays interest and curiosity about the date. Julia is confused and angered by her mother's double message.

This parental mistake is fairly common and inevitably forces the child to act contrary to the parent's *conscious* wishes. The child obeys her parent's *unconscious* demand that she misbehave.

Parents who say one thing and do another confuse and anger their children. Joseph observes his father laughing and joking about stealing expensive tools and supplies from his employer. At the same time, Joseph receives regular paternal admonitions to be honest and respect the property of others. Indeed, he is mightily punished by his father for swiping candy from the corner drugstore. Such a conflict between his father's words and deeds is bound to generate anxiety, disappointment, and confusion in Joseph. It will certainly not assist in the development of any clear commitment to the virtue of honesty.

Even with no explicit parental injunction to the contrary, parental bad example can have a powerful negative effect on conscience development. The perpetually drunken parent, though regularly contrite and apologetic after each binge, leaves his child with uncertainty about the appropriate use of alcohol. The parent also renders himself less available and less competent as a trusted teacher of values and appropriate behavior. It is highly unlikely that a child will turn to an alcoholic parent when in need.

Parents who try to teach their children by using only one level or an inappropriate level of feeling expression, whether of high or low intensity, are handicapped by their inability to teach values and to form their child's conscience. Maurice "forgets" to take out the garbage and gets a mild rebuke from his father. When Maurice takes money from his grandmother's purse and father gives him the same kind of mild rebuke, Maurice does not learn that there is a difference in severity of the two misdeeds. One mistake *feels* no different from the other. Clara, for example, complains that her mother yells at her all the time. Whether she "forgets" to make her bed before leaving for school, or whether she comes home two hours late from a date, her mother's response is the same high-pitched, intense yelling.

Both Maurice and Clara are receiving confusing messages on different levels. The relative importance of two apparently unequal acts remains in doubt. The depth of the parents' commitment to the children is left in question by the parents' bland willingness to give similar responses to very dissimilar behaviors.

If the parent hopes to give the child a well-ordered hierarchy of values, the *intensity* of his response to the child's behavior must reflect the place of a specific behavior in the total hierarchy of values.

On his way to school, Ed comes upon a friend in distress and in need of help. He has been taught by his parents to be at school on time *and* to help people in distress. Ed will almost certainly make his choice on the basis of which value, punctuality or helping your neighbor, has been taught with the most intensity by his parents.

Unavailability of a parent for establishing a trusting relationship with a child, unwillingness or inability to teach with clarity and honesty, and/or an inconsistency between parental words and deeds will all effectively prevent adequate conscience formation from developing in the child. If parents want their children to develop a strong and effective conscience, they must teach effectively. For good or for evil, the combination of what they say and what they do will teach their children the values, feelings, and behaviors which together consti-

tute conscience. If they have created a trusting, nonconflicted relationship with their child and if their own lives
are reasonably consistent with their words of instruction, they will have done all a parent can do to help
their child form a conscience.

THE CHILD'S TEMPERAMENT

Parental problems are not the only factors that interfere with conscience formation. A child may be born
with a temperament that interferes with the development of a trusting relationship with his parents.

THE DIFFICULT-TO-RAISE CHILD

In their study of delinquent adolescents, the Gluecks
found that when they were two or three years old, these
delinquents were commonly described as nonsubmis-
sive to authority, destructive, extremely restless, defiant, and stubborn.

DIFFICULT-TO-RAISE CHILDREN

Chess and Thomas identified a group of children (about
ten percent of the total) which they labeled "difficult-to-
raise." These children had very irregular biorhythms and
experienced great difficulty establishing regular sleep,
eating, and elimination patterns. One night, they would
sleep the whole night through. The next night, they
would awaken two or three times. They had irregular
eating needs. During one twenty-four hour period, they
might eat much more than the next twenty-four hours.
These "difficult" children also tended to respond to new
experiences in a negative way, usually by withdrawing.

When presented with "new" foods, they rejected or refused to eat them until repeated presentation had rendered them familiar and thus acceptable.

During periods in life when new experiences were few, the child's temperament might appear to have changed. For example, after accepting the new experience of toilet training, a child might appear to have changed temperamentally. However, when faced with the major new experience of school three years later, the child's underlying temperament might manifest itself again in the form of fear, anger, stubbornness, or other tactics aimed at avoidance of a new experience.

These "difficult" children tend to have intensely negative moods. They cry more than they laugh. They fuss more easily than they express pleasure. They are not wholly unadaptive, but simply are very slow to adjust to new situations.

While neither dull nor unresponsive, many of these children exhibit a lack of sensitivity to their environment, particularly their human environment. Paradoxically, such children may be hyperactive and seem over-responsive to their environment. However, what we actually see is their attempt to engage their environment in such a way so as to obtain an intense response. These children seem to require a highly stimulating and exciting environment, without which they feel alienated and lonely. If their parents are not unusually intense and stimulating, they are perceived as distant, unavailable, and weak.

Nurturing such children is a demanding and stressful task. Most parents feel that their love and acceptance should transform them into happy and contented children. When the desired transformation fails to materialize, they blame themselves, feeling guilty, anxious, and helpless. Often, these parents become so frustrated and distressed by their experiences that they turn their anger toward each other, or withdraw almost comletely from their child. Most children respond initially to parental withdrawal by increasing their level of protest, which in turn elicits further parental withdrawal. Eventually, the children too give up and resign themselves to alienated and lonely lives.

Parents who have one of these "difficult" children hope that school and perhaps a good peer group will help their child. However, they discover that he also has trouble learning and behaving in school. He does not learn how to make or keep friends. He continues to have a troubled relationship with his parents and therefore his conscience tends to be weak and ineffective. He does not learn the rules, values, and feelings that would help him to relate to friends, family, and others. He feels alienated and alone, and he views his parents as weak and distant, unable to provide him with a safe relationship within which he can relax. He tests other adults who supposedly have authority over his behavior and he learns that he can manipulate them, too. Teachers, principals, social workers, police, and judges all become enemies who have proven themselves unable to control him and are consequently unworthy of his trust and respect.

Because these children need intense stimulation in order to feel alive and in contact with others, they tend to seek excitement, thrills, and danger. In this way, they "numb out" their feelings of sadness, loneliness, and alienation. Without the help of a strong conscience, they drift inexorably toward delinquency, violence, and crime. Fortunately, only a small percentage of children are born with this temperament. Most are born with a temperament that easily allows the development of a good, strong conscience.

THE OVERLY SENSITIVE CHILD

At the other end of the spectrum are those overly sensitive children who are highly vulnerable to the teaching of their parents. If their parents provide a secure, predictable environment, teaching values and behaviors in a nonconflicted manner, these children develop a conscience which is a helpful guide to them in their daily lives. They can relate to people in authority without fear, and they know the rules of family, school, and community. They have the tools that enable them to work and play in the different social structures within which they must function.

However, these sensitive children develop significant problems if their parents and teachers are unaware of their specific difficulty or are unwilling to adjust their parenting to their child's particular needs. Such children tend to be too easily affected by their parents. If their parent is unconsciously hostile, the child will accept her parent's feelings about herself and will perceive herself as loathsome or unlikeable. She will not like herself.

The child with such a sensitive temperament learns her lessons too well. A single harsh "no" from a parent becomes a commandment. The child soon has learned so many "no's" that she walks a very narrow and tortuous line. Her life may become an ordeal, avoiding all those prohibited thoughts and behaviors. Dirt, noise, excitement, touching, feeling—all this becomes suspect. The child becomes fearful of her own ideas and desires. She feels there is no safe place and perhaps no safe relationship. Her conscience becomes a monster. She refuses to risk and is constantly anxious, fearful that unless she is eternally vigilant, something terrible will unexpectedly occur. Her conscience demands constant anxiety. Every situation, every person is potentially dangerous. She cannot relax. She cannot relate. Her life is an unending ordeal. Her conscience is not helpful. Indeed, it burdens her until there is little or no joy in her life.

Parents who find themselves with children who are temperamentally oversensitive to the important persons in their lives must adapt their own parenting styles to the specific needs of these children. Unless their parents recognize their unique needs and provide the special parenting they require to develop a strong but nonpunitive conscience, these children are likely to form inhibiting or punishing consciences.

FATE

An increasing number of children in our society have been so mistreated that they have difficulty trusting even the best of parents or other adults and therefore have difficulty forming a strong conscience. Very common among these are the children who have suffered the loss of a parent at an early age. Divorce is a particularly painful experience for a small child. When one loved parent inexplicably leaves a child and his family, the child suffers a profound loss and may fear abandonment or loss of the remaining parent. If Mom has to work outside the home because of the divorce and has to place her child with a babysitter or in a day-care center, the child "loses" mother, too. Clinging, whining, and downright panic become very common in such children. The child's whole attention is directed toward avoiding the loss of his mother and is thus diverted from his proper task of learning how to behave and feel in social situations.

Children who have been mistreated, neglected, or abandoned, either physically or emotionally, feel enraged because of the mistreatment, but they also experience the fear that the mistreatment or abandonment may recur. Even when placed with "good" parents who have proven themselves capable of forming strong parent/child bonds, these children have serious difficulties trusting and forming an effective conscience. They are preoccupied with emotional and physical survival in a hostile world. The niceties of conscience formation pass them by with barely a flicker of interest.

We have examined the difficulties underlying the teaching and learning of conscience. We have seen the circumstances in which conscience formation fails and we have noted that a trusting relationship between parent and child is an essential precondition for conscience formation. How do parents establish such a relationship if trust does not exist? How do they capture a temperamentally distant and manipulative child and stuff an unwanted conscience inside? How do they repair the devastation of a painful loss so that their child is receptive to their care and instruction?

Growth, change, and development are basic to a child. Children are programmed for change. There are very few children who cannot develop a trusting relationship to a parent if that parent is determined to succeed. Even the most difficult child can learn how to behave and how to feel the necessary guilt and remorse. The pain and anguish of a loss can be relieved by parents who can empathize and engage those feelings which interfere with learning the lessons of conscience formation. Parents can and must teach their children to trust, to feel, and to behave.

Discipline is the most intense, explicit, and successful form of teaching conscience. As we have learned, some forms of discipline are more successful than others. The One-Minute Scolding is an effective discipline precisely because it focuses on and causes the development of a trusting relationship. It compels both parent and child to engage in that process we call relating, bonding, or attachment. Firm, consistent, kind, and intense discipline can be the beginning and the foundation of a trusting parent-child relationship and the formation of a strong conscience. Because it both depends upon and promises an intense, trusting relationship, the One-Minute Scolding must be given by a significant adult. Ordinarily, only parents or parent substitutes can promise a child such a relationship. Teachers, probation officers, and counselors can be helpful and supportive to their pupils and charges, but they cannot promise these children an enduring and trusting relationship.

The One-Minute Scolding is not a panacea. It will not cure troubled parents or resolve marriage problems. It alone will not make a child happy or secure in his new foster home. The One-Minute Scolding is a simple way to begin a new discipline and a new relationship. It seems to work despite parental problems. The One-Minute Scolding is an effective discipline *if it is used*.

The simplicity of the One-Minute Scolding and its easy applicability to most disciplinary situations allows even the most troubled parent to use it successfully. Indifferent or troubled parents may have difficulty initiating the One-Minute Scolding because their child's needs may not be uppermost in their minds. These parents will require much encouragement and support from their friends and other adults to begin and persevere in their discipline. Our experience with troubled parents has convinced us that they can and will use the One-Minute Scolding as effective discipline for their children if given adequate direction and encouragement. If they can be encouraged and supported to use the One-Minute Scolding in a friendly and consistent manner, they are invariably rewarded by significant and almost immediate improvement in their child's behavior. Often, troubled parents have few pleasures or successes in their lives and they find success with their children particularly rewarding. Their marriage may have failed and they may feel overwhelmed by their problems, but, if their rebellious nine-year-old or their stubborn three-year-old responds to them positively, their life becomes much more pleasant.

Parents who give their children conflicting messages as to what is right and what is wrong must resolve these conflicts before they use the One-Minute Scolding. Mothers and fathers need to agree on what is proper behavior and what is not. A child does not need numerous rules but a few explicit and clear-cut commands. When a child misbehaves, he must be confronted with that mistake in a kind but firm manner. Mother, father, and child must all know what is a mistake and what is not. Both parents must be willing to discipline their child when he needs discipline. He needs discipline (teaching) whenever he breaks a rule.

There is nothing magical about the One-Minute Scolding. If one parent uses it to discipline her child for misbehaving and the other parent unconsciously rewards the child for the same behavior, the child will still be confused as to what his parents want him to learn.

For children who have developed an "internal barrier" to the feelings of others, the One-Minute Scolding is the most effective and, in some cases, the only effective discipline. Children who have been taught to rely on themselves for help and children born with the "difficult-to-raise" temperament have "numbed out" their own feelings and in the same process have become insensitive to the feelings of others. These children require intense expressions of feelings from the scolding parent to penetrate the "feeling barrier." Such scoldings must not be overlong lest the child have time to marshall his defenses and keep the parent and the parent's feelings at a distance. Immediately after the short intense scolding, the parent dramatically relaxes and becomes tender and loving. In that brief moment when the child's psyche scrambles to adjust to the different parental message, the warmth and caring of the parent floods the child.

Initially, the child manages to distance himself quickly from the parent's loving words and attention. He is suspicious and guarded, suspecting some sort of trickery. As the child experiences more and more scoldings over the weeks and months, he gradually allows more and more of the warmth and caring of the parent to touch him. With this openness to the parent's love comes the learning of the lesson. Though the child may not put his thoughts into words, even to himself, nevertheless he moves through an internal process which goes something like this:

> "Mother gets angry when I disobey her. She reminds me every time I forget to obey her. She also tells me how much she loves me, and she tells me nice things about myself. I love my mother. I don't want to make her angry."

These children can respond and change their behavior quickly. However, their conscience development is slow and uneven, even with the consistent use of the One-Minute Scolding. They tend to be "flexible" and may appear to be compliant and docile when confronted by parents who are using a new and unfamiliar discipline. However, several months of consistent discipline will be necessary before signs of conscience are regularly seen.

Children who have been neglected and mistreated, and especially those who have been "abandoned" several times, seem to respond to the One-Minute Scolding when they respond to no other discipline. The conscience of such a child has not developed because the child has put all of his energy and abilities into protecting himself from further mistreatment or another abandonment. He does not trust his parents. Values and behaviors can be adopted if they seem to protect him from danger or loss. But they will be just as easily abandoned if they seem no longer useful in preventing pain or loss.

These children feel alone and alienated. They have great difficulty *feeling* the parent's love and concern. Conscience-forming messages from the parents are heard but very little feeling is attached to them by the child. In such children, conscience formation can occur only when the parent delivers the message with great intensity of feeling and then rewards the child for listening with equally intense expressions of tenderness and caring. The parents must use their bodies, particularly their hands, to express these feelings to their child. In the first half of the scolding, they communicate their intense feelings of anger using their face, body, and gestures as well as their words. They then touch, stroke, and fondle their child, telling him also through body language that they care deeply for him. Few children can long resist if the parents repeatedly engage them in this attachment process.

Children who are temperamentally insensitive to their human environment and children who have had parents with a single level of feeling-response to their misbehaviors, respond well to the One-Minute Scolding if the scolding is given with appropriate feeling by the parents. Temperamentally insensitive children absolutely require scoldings that begin with an intense discharge of the parent's feelings.

"I am so angry with you, I could grind you to powder!"

The child must *feel* his parent's feelings so that his focus of attention is narrowed and directed toward that parent. He must not be allowed to distance himself and observe. When the feelings of the parent dramatically change, the child is remarkably vulnerable and open to them. The parent rewards the child with love and tenderness. The rule, the limit, and the value enter the

child's memory along with the warmth and tenderness. Conscience formation progresses slowly but surely.

The One-Minute Scolding can also be used quite effectively with overly sensitive children, but their parents need to remember that their strong feelings have a very powerful impact on this child. These parents must modulate their feelings to a level which will not overwhelm their child. Fewer scoldings with less intense feelings, but with very clear and consistent messages, will facilitate the development of a very adequate conscience in these children.

What do parents look for in children as signs of conscience formation? In the first stage, they will detect that the child *knows* he has made a mistake, that he is *aware* of what is right and what is wrong. However, he may not yet be anxious about the wrongness of the deed so much as worried about the possibility of getting caught.

In the next stage, parents will notice that their child not only knows when he makes a mistake, but *feels* bad about it as well. Guilty behavior and remorse now are likely to follow a misdeed and, in general, a marked decrease in misbehaviors should become evident over an extended period of time. Unfortunately, this is the stage of conscience formation when many parents relax and turn their attention to other, perhaps more urgent matters. They are not aware that their child's conscience remains fragile and undeveloped and that they must continue to devote time and energy to their child's developing conscience.

In the next phase of conscience formation, parents will notice that their child has become aware that his behavior affects the trusting relationship he has with them. No longer does the child fear only his parent's punitive response to his mistakes, he is *aware* and *regrets* that his behavior has an affect on their relationship.

"When I hit my little sister, my Mommie gets mad. When Mommie gets mad, I get scared. She might go away!"

Parents may see only the child's attempt to restore his relationship with them. He may ask for forgiveness or do something which will please or placate them. He fears their displeasure and is aware that his misdeed has caused the loss of the important feeling of security and trust which should characterize all parent-child relationships.

Finally, when conscience formation is well advanced, the parents may note that the child becomes anxious at just the thought of committing a forbidden act. His conscience has expanded beyond simply knowing what is right and wrong and that his parents will become upset with him if he misbehaves. Now, when he makes a mistake, he experiences an inner sense of *estrangement from his idea of who he is:*

"I'm not the sort of person who does that kind of thing."

The child's relationship to his parents has developed so that he feels close to them and he no longer fears that he has no one to turn to when in need. When faced with a moral problem, he recalls the teaching of his parents and their feelings about similar problems he has encountered in the past. He may compare his anticipated behavior with his own expectations of himself. He is motivated not only by a fear of losing the trusting relationship he now has with his parents but also by a true sense of what is right. He also has a sense that he is a person who does the right thing.

Conscience formation is a matter of critical importance for the individual, the family, and society. It is a long-term process of teaching by the parent based upon a trusting relationship between parent and child. Effective and consistent discipline is a vital component of that teaching. The One-Minute Scolding is a particularly effective discipline for troubled children and parents because it not only disciplines but it also engages both parent and child in the development of a trusting relationship which is the root of a healthy conscience.

7

From Eighteen Months to Eighteen Years: A Scolding for All Seasons

This chapter is not meant to be a cookbook for scolding. The examples we use are rather general. Because children and parents in real life bring a huge variety of possibilities and idiosyncrasies to a crisis, your personal expression in a scolding is not likely to match to these examples exactly.

It is also important to remember that the One-Minute Scolding as a disciplinary procedure can be begun and applied at any point in the development of a child. In other words, just because your youngster is already fourteen, it does not mean that it is too late to have a real impact on his behavior and effect a change.

What this chapter wants to point out is that the general *form* of the One-Minute Scolding remains the same, but the *tone* and *intensity* varies:

- with the age of the child
- the temperament of the child
- the severity of the misdeed

THAT'S A NO NO

At eighteen months, Susanna is bright and inquisitive, and the TV dials are a fascination to her. Although it is not dangerous to play with the dials, it is an annoyance to have to readjust the set each time one wants to watch the news. So her parents have made a rule that is important to them. Most everything that is dangerous to the baby has already been removed, locked up, or in some way baby-proofed. Not playing with dials is one of the few rules that they wish to teach Susanna. Susanna knows this.

One morning, Susanna toddles up to the television set and begins to play with the dials. Her mother can tell that Susanna knows this may be forbidden because she looks expectantly at her mother as she fiddles with the controls.

The mother quietly says, "No."

Susanna looks at her mother but continues to play with the dials.

Her mother repeats, "Susanna, no. Go away from the television set!"

Susanna's eyes widen and she watches her mother very carefully, but she does not leave the set. She keeps her fingers on the dial. Susanna is disobeying her mama.

If a child does not learn to obey her parents, she frequently misunderstands her power, controls the family, and becomes "the boss." A family "bossed" by a small child is a family in considerable distress. So her mother uses the One-Minute Scolding. But because Susanna is very young, the scolding must be short, and the feelings expressed not so intense as to overwhelm her.

Susanna's mother approaches and says firmly: "No! No, you may not play with the television set, Susanna."

When the mother says "No," she may shake her finger or frown at Susanna to communicate her disapproval visually. The voice and gestures are forceful enough, so Susanna will feel a little frightened. The mother sees Susanna become a bit tearful and her lower lip trembles. Perhaps she drops her head and her body sags. That marks the end of the first half of the One-Minute Scolding. It may not have lasted ten seconds.

The mother then picks Susanna up, holds her closely and warmly and says, "Susanna, I love you. You are a sweet child. I don't want you to play with the TV. That is a No-no. Mama loves you but Mama does not want you to play with the TV." As Susanna quiets down, her mother turns and points to the television saying gently, "Susanna, that's a No. The television is a No. I do not want you to play with it." Susanna's mother takes her from the television and interests her in something else.

Susanna is alert and responsive, but one scolding may not be enough to establish that fiddling with the television is forbidden. Most likely, Susanna will try to play with the dials again. Perhaps this time, Susanna's father sees that she is playing with it. For the sake of consistency, it is important for children that either parent could discipline them when they break a rule. These parents have agreed that they both will help Susanna with this rule. As Susanna looks uncertainly at her father, she reaches out and plays with one of the dials. Immediately her father goes up and, in a stern voice and manner, says, "No! The television set is a No."

Susanna drops to the floor, wailing as though she had been spanked. The first half of the scolding is over. Her father picks her up and comforts her. As soon as she can respond to him, he directs her gaze towards the television and says, "The TV is a No; you may not play with the TV set." He is warm and comforting. "I love you, Susanna, you are a good little girl. I know you can learn not to play with the TV."

Then, he too takes Susanna to another place where she will not be tempted to play with the television again.

This scenario may need to be repeated several times. Each episode takes no more than ten to fifteen seconds. The child will learn very quickly not to play with the TV set. There is no need to spank fingers, nor is it wise to put the TV set out of reach. Most children can learn quickly to leave things alone if they are consistently and effectively disciplined to do so.

THE EXPLORER

Now we apply the One-Minute Scolding to a four-year-old who likes to explore and visit the neighbors. Little David has been playing quietly in the garage with the door open. His mother knows there is nothing in the garage that he could get into that could hurt him, so she is in the garden planting.

At some point his mother becomes aware that David is no longer nearby. She finds him in the neighbor's garage with his four-year-old friend, Troy. They are playing "gas station" and are filling the gas tank of the automobile with water from the garden hose. David's mother recognizes the extreme danger immediately. They have flushed out gasoline and it has spilled onto the garage floor. If ignited, the gasoline would envelop both boys and the entire garage in flames.

She grabs both boys, literally dragging them out of danger, she alerts Troy's parents, and calls the fire department. Only after ten minutes of frantic activity does she turn her attention to David.

David and Troy are fascinated by all the activity, especially by the fire engines. They had already forgotten that they were responsible for all this excitement. So when David's mother gets around to disciplining David, he is unprepared for her anger. Kneeling so that she is face-to-face with David, she holds him firmly by both shoulders. She knows that she must teach him *never* to play that game again. She may not have a second chance.

"David, you've made a terrible mistake! I am very upset with you! Playing with gasoline is *dangerous!* I don't want you ever to do that again. You could have started a fire and burned yourself terribly. You must *never, ever* play with gasoline again."

There is no doubt that David's mother is extremely upset. He can feel the agitation in her voice, in the hold that she has on his shoulders, and in her body posture and language. Small children are very responsive to strong feelings in their parents and David is no exception. He responds by crying.

His mother folds him into her arms. Perhaps she weeps with him, discharging her anxiety. Through her tears she tells David, "David, I love you so much. If anything ever happened to you, I would be so upset. You are a wonderful boy but you must be careful. You must never play with gasoline again. I want to be such a good mama. I have to teach you not to do things like that. You must not do dangerous things like that. I love you so much that I am going to scold you every time you make a mistake."

David stops his crying. He is aware that his mother is no longer angry but is earnest and intense. Now she makes David look at her directly. She asks, "David, why am I upset with you?"

David replies, "I played gas station with gasoline."

"Are you ever going to do that again?"

"No, Mama," says David.

"David tell me, 'Mama, I won't play with gasoline again."

David responds, "Mama, I won't play with gasoline again."

David's mother takes him by the hand and together they return home. The scolding is over. We hope David will never need another lesson about the dangers of gasoline.

Parents must teach children to avoid what is dangerous. It is their responsibility to protect them from danger, as well as to teach them how to avoid those dangers themselves. A child quickly learns that some mistakes are more serious than others if the parent's emotional response varies. When children put themselves in truly dangerous situations, parents must respond with strong, vigorous feelings in contrast to mild disappointment at the child's difficulty in learning table manners or other skills which are not so vital. In very serious matters, children need to learn their lesson the first time. There may be no second chance.

A STRONG PARENT CAN BE TRUSTED TO HANDLE MONSTERS

Teresa is six. She has been having nightmares and waking up two or three times a night. She cries and refuses to be consoled unless one of her parents stays in her room or she is allowed to sleep with them in their bed. The nightmares began the day Teresa's mother was delayed for half an hour and Teresa had to wait at school. She had cried and was afraid she was forgotten. Although the incident had not been her fault, Teresa's mother felt guilty. She felt she should have been there on time, so that Teresa would not have been so frightened. It was, therefore, easy for Teresa to manipulate

her mother into allowing her to sleep in mother and father's bed.

After a telephone consultation with Teresa's pediatrician, her parents decided to make Teresa stay in her own bed, even if she is frightened. The next time Teresa appears at her parents' bedroom door looking forlorn and frightened, her mother responds in a firm voice and says, "Teresa, go back to bed."

Teresa begins to cry and says, "But I'm scared. There's a monster in my closet." Teresa's mother gets up, takes Teresa back to her room and says, "Well, let's see." They both go to the closet and look. Teresa's mother does not try to prove that there are no monsters, by turning on the lights, etc. She wisely realizes that the "monsters" of Teresa's fantasies are as real to Teresa and just as frightening as any visible monster might be. Those things that go "bump in the night" are the unexpressed angers and fears of her daytime experiences.

But for now the lesson Teresa must learn is twofold. She is to ask for help when she needs comfort. She will not have to handle such strong feelings by herself. But she is also to remain in her own bed. Mother, not Teresa, is in control. The monster has apparently fled. Then mother tucks Teresa into her own bed, gives her a hug and says, "Teresa, I know you are scared. But Mommy and Daddy are here and all you have to do is call me and I'll help you. If any monster scares you, I can deal with him easily. Now, you go to sleep. If you wake up afraid, you may call me for help. But stay in your bed."

Teresa is not happy. She was afraid of that monster in her closet. Furthermore, she does not trust that her mother or father will protect her. After all, she was forgotten at school. She tries to sleep but her fear returns and becomes greater and greater. Finally, she gets up and dashes to her mother and father's bed and tries to climb in between them. That's such a warm and safe place.

Her mother wakes up. Quietly, but firmly, she takes Teresa back to her own room. She sits down on Teresa's bed, and puts Teresa on her lap.

"Teresa, I am angry with you. I know you are afraid that there may be another monster in your closet. I am angry with you because you don't trust me. You don't think that I know how to take care of that monster. I can. If you call me I'll come in and help you. But you disobeyed me and got out of bed again. I am scolding you because you didn't call me. You disobeyed me and got into my bed. That bed is for Daddy and me. Your bed is for you. You may not sleep with me in my bed. I get very angry with you when you do not obey me. If you are worried or frightened, just call Daddy or me and one of us will come. I am very angry with you, Teresa."

The mother continues until she knows Teresa has begun to learn her lesson. Teresa weeps. Her mother changes her way of holding Teresa and is soft and accepting. "You are a sweet girl. I know you are afraid. I will protect you and I will take care of you. That's the job of Mommies and Daddies. I love you so much that I have to scold you when you don't obey. I'm going to scold you every time you make a mistake like that because I love you. I want to be such a good mommy for you. I want you to grow up to be a big strong girl. You must trust me and you must obey me.

"Don't worry, I'll help you. Every time you forget and don't trust me, I'll scold you. Soon you will understand that you must call me when you're worried or scared."

Her mother then begins the next part of the scolding and asks,

"Teresa, why am I scolding you?"

"Because I climbed into your bed. Instead I should call you."

"Yes, Teresa. Every time you make a mistake like that, I'm going to scold you because I love you and I want to be a good mommy for you. Do you understand?"

Teresa nods. Her mother gives her a warm hug, helps Teresa back into bed, tucks her in and goes back to her own bedroom. If Teresa again forgets and crawls into bed with her parents she will have another scolding until she knows that Mother or Father will not relent and allow her to sleep in their bed. But her parents will insist that Teresa ask them to help her with her fear.

Teresa's anger and fear of being abandoned arose out of the incident when she was not picked up in time from school. Sometimes those things happen. But when parents are strong, consistent, and warm, they prove they can be trusted not to abandon a child. Furthermore, a strong parent can be trusted to handle closet monsters easily.

"LATE FOR DINNER, AGAIN"

Peter is ten. He practices soccer just about every afternoon and has been coming home late for dinner despite instruction from his parents that he is to be home by five-thirty.

His family is well into dinner when he arrives home happy and flushed. He is at least forty-five minutes late. Obviously, he has lost track of the time again.

Peter's father gets up and says, "Peter, let's go into your bedroom. I have to scold you."

Peter's face falls. He follows his father into the bedroom and tries to explain why he was delayed.

"No excuses, Peter. You have a watch and you know

we expect you home by five-thirty." The father doesn't let Peter argue. He sternly holds Peter's shoulder, looks at him, and scolds.

"Peter, I am very angry with you. You were supposed to be home at five-thirty and it is now six-twenty. You are late and I am angry with you. I am really upset, Peter. And we all get worried. We have warned you repeatedly and you seem not to hear us. You know the rule that we eat our meals all together. There is no excuse for you not to be here on time. Your soccer practice is over at quarter-to-five and we have allowed you plenty of time to josh around with your friends and still be home by five-thirty. Yesterday, you told me that you understood, you told us all that you would be home by five-thirty at the latest, and you forgot again. I really am furious with you, Peter."

Peter is shaken. He had forgotten. He remembers

clearly that his parents had warned him that he must be home by five-thirty. For some reason, he just did not remember. He had enjoyed the soccer and playing with his friends. He had enjoyed talking with them and fooling around with his bike after practice and he had truly forgotten his promise to be home at five-thirty. He feels terrible. His father gets mad as heck with him and when that happens, it's scary to look at his father.

The father sees that Peter is sad and a little frightened. His grip on Peter's shoulder softens. His tone of voice softens.

"Peter, I love you a lot. You are a fine son. I care heaps about you. In fact, I'm scolding you because I love you, because I care about you. Especially, I want to be a good father to you. I'm scolding you because you made a thoughtless mistake. You promised you'd be home by five-thirty so that we could eat our evening meal together. I know you forgot and didn't do it on purpose. But I surely hope that this scolding will help you remember tomorrow night. Because, if you forget again, I'm going to scold you again. I won't forget.

"In fact, it's easy for me to scold you, Peter, because that is what a loving dad does for his kids. Every time you make a mistake like this, every time you forget and don't obey, I'll scold you. That's just to help you. It's no big deal, Peter. O.K.?"

Peter nods. His head is lowered and he looks subdued. "Why will I scold you? What are you to remember?" His father asks him quickly for the lesson learned and Peter has the message.

His father gives him a warm hug and says, "O.K., Peter, let's go eat dinner and we won't talk any more about it."

"O.K.. Dad, I'll remember next time."

We all forget and Peter is no exception. So there is no

need to make Peter stop playing soccer, or to humiliate him, or spank him, or isolate him from the rest of the family. Peter's parents are happy that he plays soccer and has his friends. But of course they also want him to learn to obey and respond to their wishes. They feel strongly about the importance of mealtimes as family times, as a pleasant opportunity to share stories and reestablish ties. Soccer and family dinners do not have to cancel each other out.

If Peter forgets again, his parents' feelings will increase in intensity and should be expressed in the One-Minute Scolding. Before long, Peter will remember to be home for dinner.

POT IS FORBIDDEN

Fourteen-year-old Agatha has never been a problem. She does well in school, has friends, and generally is a thoughtful child in her family. So, her mother is surprised and upset when, one day, Agatha comes home from school with red eyes and cheeks flushed, looking very guilty, and smelling of marijuana. Agatha has given in to peer pressure or to her curiosity about pot. At her school, pot is used by many of her peers.

Her parents have often discussed with the children their concerns about marijuana, tobacco, alcohol, and other drugs. Agatha always agreed with their principles. She seemed to understand and agree with their explanation of why drugs must be avoided. So this mother is amazed and shocked that Agatha could do something so "out of character."

As a good parent, Agatha's mother deals with the problem immediately and honestly. She will not postpone the issue until her husband gets back and though such a disturbing problem has not come up with her other children, she is determined to engage it immediately.

She says, "Agatha, come with me to the den." Her voice is stern and intense. Agatha knows she is in trouble. She goes off with her mother and stands with head hung down and shoulders slumped forward. "Agatha, you have been smoking marijuana. I am terribly angry with you. We have been very clear with you, both your father and I, about the use of such drugs. Marijuana can be harmful. It is illegal and utterly forbidden. We don't want you to put harmful substances in your body. Actually, Agatha, I am so utterly surprised at you. I really cannot believe that you gave in to some of those kids and smoked marijuana. I figured you were strong enough to withstand that kind of group thinking. There are countless other ways to share friendships without jeopardizing your health and safety. Pot is a dumb cop-out, Agatha, as far as I'm concerned. If life feels difficult for kids at fourteen, it's for parents to be helpful by taking a strong position. Pot would be a stupid way to skip out of the feelings that are common at your age. I am so angry with you, Agatha."

Her mother's voice is intensely angry and disappointed. Agatha feels terrible. She realizes she's made a bad mistake. Actually, she knew that her mother and father would be very upset with her if she tried marijuana. Agatha starts to cry.

At once her mother stops the angry scolding. She gathers Agatha into her arms and holds her tight. "Agatha, I love you so awfully much. I think you are a wonderful person. You hardly ever are a worry to us. Actually, you give us a lot of joy. Your schoolwork is good, you are kind, thoughtful, and responsible. I admire you. At your age, I realize how important it is to be part of the group and that you'd be curious about pot. Kids just are curious about new things. I suppose it doesn't look to you like pot is hurting any of those other kids. But, I want you to stay away from it. Your dad and I feel that smoking marijuana is harmful."

She knows Agatha is feeling sad and guilty about doing something that was clearly forbidden. She finishes the last half of the scolding with a hug, saying, "Look Agatha, I don't want you to smoke marijuana. I don't want you to smoke tobacco, drink alcohol, or take drugs. You make a mistake if you think those substances can't harm you. Is it clear to you? I want to be a good mom and do a good job. This is all I'm going to say. I don't want you to do it again. If you make a mistake again like that what can you expect from me? I will scold you again. You must remember, no matter what, I love you."

Actually, Agatha is relieved. Her parents have stood by their values, and it makes her feel safe and secure knowing that they stick up for their values—always have and always will. She does worry what her father will think when he learns that she's tried pot, but she knows that he will not scold her. She has been scolded already and the discipline is over.

BE HOME BY MIDNIGHT

Mark is seventeen. He has made a contract with his parents: he may use the family car to go to the football game and dance if he is home by midnight. He has also agreed that if he runs into any problems and expects to be late, he will call. He dashes out, happy about the evening ahead. His parents, however, feel pangs of worry. Mark is bright, sensible, and even thoughtful, but like any teenager, he's occasionally shown lapses in judgment. Sometimes he does very dumb things. This is not because he is indifferent, stupid, or uncaring, but because his judgment is not always mature. He is a good driver, but he tends to show off with his friends and has had to be reminded to drive within the speed limit. His parents know how important it is for teenagers to be able to drive. Besides, there's no way for him to get around this big city without a car. Bus connections are impossible at night. But the thought of his driving the car on the crowded Friday night freeway fills them with anxiety.

Midnight comes and goes. Twelve-thirty—one o'clock—both parents are frantic. They can't erase thoughts of squealing brakes, ambulances, flashing lights, hospital emergency rooms. The anxiety engenders anger.

At one-fifteen, just as they consider calling the police, they hear his car enter the driveway. There he is. Their anxiety transforms into a full-blown rage. Mark opens the door and is met by two furious parents. It's clear enough. He knows he has made a serious mistake.

"Mark, you really blew it. You really made a bad mistake!" Dad grabs him by the shoulder and scolds in a loud and agitated voice. He reminds him of their agreement. He tells Mark how worried and angry they have been. Mark listens to him and feels guilty and a little sad. He knows he's made a bad mistake. Then his dad abruptly makes the transition from loud scolding to being warm and concerned. Now Mark really feels terrible.

"Mark, your mom and I love you a lot. We care so much for you. We were terrified that you'd made some error in judgment and had had an accident. We want you to use the car, even though we are a bit anxious when you do. We want you to be able to go out and have a good time with your friends. We know you are a sensible and thoughtful driver, but when you are late and don't call, we become worried and angry. Every possible accident races through our minds and we sit here scared and helpless."

"Look, we are scolding you because we hate feeling so terrified. You know you can call us to say you'll be late. There is no reason whatsoever why you cannot assure us that you are safe and that there's a reason for being late. We expect you to honor your agreements. You promised us that you would call us if you couldn't be home by midnight."

Mark felt uncomfortable while his parents were scolding him, but he could cope with their anger and disappointment. It was when they abruptly became warm and caring and loving to him that he became so extremely uncomfortable that all he wanted to do was escape. He felt ashamed that he did not phone. When they both gave him a brief hug and sent him to bed, he was immensely relieved.

Teenagers are especially uncomfortable with the second half of the scolding. The first half is easier to cope with; it's easier to agree that they were mistaken than it is to be defined as some "great kid." Most teenagers learn quickly that to avoid the discomfort of the second half of the scolding, they have to obey their parents and keep those rules that they know in their hearts are reasonable.

8

Kids Have Their Own Ploys

Charming and docile as they may be, your children are not going to roll over and play dead when you scold them. They have a whole arsenal of clever defenses, so you had better be prepared for some "creative" responses.

Let's look in on some scenes of parents scolding their children, paying particular attention to the defenses the child will use and what the parent may do to "neutralize" those defenses.

WIGGLING

Some small children squirm and wiggle and slip out of your lap like a fish to the floor. The scolding cannot begin until parent and children are firmly settled in. The child is testing your conviction and your strength.

You don't need to work out with weights to be strong enough for this youngster. It is exactly the slippery fish who needs to be held on your lap. Through age six or seven, the scolding is best begun with the child on your lap. Here's what you need to do. It will not hurt the youngster nor break her spirit. It will only relieve her to know that you are indeed strong enough to handle her.

Grasp her by the upperarms, place her on your lap, lock her in place by putting your leg over hers, hold her hands, and get on with the scolding.

HOWLING

Some youngsters may cry and wail and scream as though they were being beaten—and all you did so far was begin your scolding! It may cause your spouse to run in, alarmed. But no one is hurt.

You will not want to start a screaming match to have your scolding heard over the din. Instead, surprise him by giving him permission to do exactly what he is already doing. "Go ahead, Matt. You feel bad and you should feel bad. So I want you to cry, very hard. Get it out of your system. I'll just hold you and wait. When you finish, I'll go on with the scolding."

Matt may find it difficult to carry on and on with loud howls just to delay what is going to happen anyway. After all, you are still holding him and it is clear that you are willing to wait for three days if you have to. His out-of-proportion shrieking will not ruffle your patience nor drown your determination. Neither have you set yourself up for another match with him as to "who is the boss around here." Had you fallen for his ploy and demanded silence so that he could hear your scolding, you would only escalate the match which, indeed, you would probably lose. Save yourself the frustration. Insist that he wail louder and he will find himself an obedient son, howling at your command. Or, more likely, he will quiet down.

When you know he can now hear you, proceed with the scolding. If it is necessary for Matt to check your determination and patience again with another crack at wailing, encourage him. "Go ahead, Matt, you still feel awful. Cry as hard as you need to. Get it out of your system." When he is finished you resume your scolding, just where you left off. Matt isn't stupid. He will see that his behavior has only prolonged the inevitable. Besides, it's a great relief to him to know that you mean to hang in there.

SHUTTING OUT

Marianna sits on her mother's lap and is being scolded. Suddenly, she is inspired to put her fingers in her ears and squeeze her eyes shut. She does not like what she hears and sees. You take her fingers out of her ears very calmly, and hold her hands in yours. You know you cannot open her eyes. Marianna turns her face away,

squeezes her eyes shut even tighter and pulls as far away from you as she can. No problem. Marianna can still hear you even if she cannot see you.

So proceed with your scolding, first the angry part and then the part that tells her how you love her and want her not to misbehave anymore. Your message will come through loud and clear. She will hear the feelings in your voice and feel them in your hug. Marianna will know you are loving and strong enough to cope with her attempts to avoid discipline. You have promised her that you will always scold her when she makes a mistake, no matter what, and you will always love her, no matter what.

APPARENT INDIFFERENCE

Ella Mae is nine years old and tough. It has come to her father's attention that she has told a bold-faced lie. He begins his scolding and though he is really quite irritated and angry and his voice clearly expresses it, Ella Mae has focused her gaze coolly some place in the area of his tie pin and remains totally unruffled.

Were you Ella Mae's father, remember, persevere. No need to get frantic and raise your voice. Remain exactly as angry as you feel and proceed with the scolding. Ella Mae's cool inperturbability is designed to make you feel ineffectual. Believe me, if she can hear you, she is having intense feelings.

As the scolding is concluded with the warm promise of care and helpfulness, her father gives her a hug, and suddenly Ella Mae bursts into tears.

"No one loves me," she sobs. Suddenly, there is a discharge of feeling and the little girl shows how very sad she really has been feeling. The stony, glazed look was her effort to keep all this sadness locked in where no one would touch it. Her father is present and ready with his warmth and understanding.

FEELING MISTREATED

Ian, who is eleven, has taken twenty dollars from his visiting grandmother's purse. You are very angry and upset with him. Your scolding states this clearly and furthermore, there is restitution to be made. In the scolding you offer a very clear plan as to how this restitution is to be made, and you also promise to help him carry it out.

"Ian, because I love you and want to help you solve this problem, I will advance you the twenty dollars to

pay grandma back. We will go to grandma together and I will give you courage to ask her forgiveness and tell her it won't happen again."

The scolding is not yet finished and Ian interrupts with the complaint that he's always getting all the scoldings in this house, that you never scold his sister. He tries to convince you that he is the family scapegoat and make you feel guilty.

Do not deal with any of this material until after the scolding is complete. After the hug, encourage him to talk about his feelings of being mistreated. Encourage him to say how sad and angry he must feel for being scolded more often than his sister.

Do not tell him that he must not have those feelings, or that it is wrong to feel mistreated. Listen carefully without interruption and encourage him to discharge everything until he is finished.

"Ian, it's too bad you feel so mistreated. I'm sorry and I certainly don't want to be unfair. But I will scold you every time you misbehave, because I love you and want to be a helpful mom. If you misbehave more often than Tricia, you'll have to be scolded more often. If I ever scold you for anything other than misbehavior or a broken rule, please tell me. I surely want to be fair with you, Ian."

PRESSING YOUR BUTTONS AND VERBAL RETORTS

Phillip is a powerful player. He needs a scolding even if he is a strapping thirteen. He left the garage in a mess and the agreement was made that this Saturday it was his turn to straighten things up and sweep. Instead, he took off with his buddies for the afternoon. Later, he saunters into the kitchen and his mother catches him by the sleeve, holds his arm, and tells him he's due for a One-Minute Scolding. She feels a little awkward about the formula but takes a breath to begin when Phillip is inspired to cash in on her awkward feelings.

"Great," he says, "I love this. The boiled egg scolding, leaves ya a little soft in the head but. . . . Could I get you a timer, perhaps your little recipe book so that you do me just right, not too hard, not too runny. Mom, you've got to be kidding. This is one big waste of time."

His mother interrupts, "It certainly is, Phillip. If you'll save your words for afterwards, you'll not prolong the minute. I'll be glad to hear how angry you are when I'm finished, but your sarcasm won't protect you from getting a scolding. . . ."

Proceed and complete the entire scolding. Afterwards, invite his feelings.

EMANCIPATING

When teenagers practice their independence they may try breaking a rule here and there. But pretending to be fully emancipated does not mean that there are no consequences for those broken rules.

As the mother or father, one cannot afford to "look the other way." Your authority is being directly challenged, but remember, down deep, your teenager does not want you to relinquish it, no matter how testy he or she is.

Karen, at sixteen, has just arrived home an hour-and-a-half late from an excursion with the family car.

Both parents stand at the door to receive her. As Karen knows what to expect, she pushes past them defiantly and heads down the hallway to her room saying, "Look,

I don't need any of your lectures and scoldings. I'd much rather you just told me to stay home instead of going through all this stuff."

No problem. Her parents trundle off down the hall behind her. Her father begins the scolding as they walk toward her room. If she interrupts again with sarcasm, ridicule, or defiance, they simply wait until she finishes and then proceed with the scolding. Her dad knows not to get caught in a shouting match, so as Karen raises her voice dramatically, her dad just responds ever more quietly. When the minute is up, each parent again reminds Karen how much they love her and leave quietly. The scolding is over.

More than anything else, children want to be absolutely certain that you are strong enough for them and love them enough to stand by them. No matter what kind of defenses your youngsters use, you will reach them effectively if you are absolutely firm in your delivery and completion of the One-Minute Scolding. Deliver it exactly as prescribed, thirty seconds of high-level negative feeling, a deep breath, then the abrupt downhill course of thirty seconds that are just as intensely warm, loving, supportive, and present. Courage. Persistence pays off.

9 The Importance of No

We talk so often of being positive. We even speak of the One-Minute Scolding as being "positive discipline," but the One-Minute Scolding does have its negative side—its angry, negative feeling side. What is good about the One-Minute Scolding is the fact that it is whole, complete, and, though it is a scolding, it ends with positive feelings. It is positive in its net effect. It affirms the child. It is this balance of positive and negative that we wish to consider.

Today many people have trouble with negative feelings, trouble with anger, and trouble expressing anger. We are so afraid to hear the negative or be negative that saying a clear, crisp "no" feels impossible. "Will you volunteer to work on the school auction?" "Well, let me see, I'd really love to, but I'm not sure I'm free. . . ."

"Mommy thinks you'd better stop playing in the sand now. She wants you to have your bath. If you don't come in soon. . . ." "You've got to accentuate the positive, eliminate the negative, latch on to the affirmative. . . ." But by eliminating the negative we've actually created "Mr. Inbetween."

"No!" "No" is a word with rights equal to "yes." Its meaning is different, but its value is utterly equal to that positive word "yes."

Two-year-olds have none of this prejudice. They can say "no" with authority. This word is useful to them. It is the ultimate expression of their budding autonomy, and mothers hate it. The "terrible twos," we call that stage. It is that time when mother and child are thrust into opposite camps. Does emancipation have to be won? Certainly. But does so much of it have it to be fraught with anger, fear, and danger? Imagine if parents came to enjoy that early symbolic gesture of autonomy in their toddlers? What might happen if "no" lost its battle cry status and became a word, used first by the parent with the same authority and definition but without anger? What if "no" should lose its association with fear, anger, ambivalence, or anxiety?

While grandma's house may abound with "no-no's"— the boston fern, the trinkets on the coffee table, the stair railings, and the detergents under the sink—at home, "no" can be centered on a few, easy-to-apply areas.

"No" is a legitimate, negative fact of life, so it can be taught with validity which need not be fraught with anger or fear. "No" can become a game in which the parent teaches the negative facts of life with certainty. "No" can be slow and gentle, it can be laughed and sung, and chuckled and danced. It can be loving and it can be associated with the joy and concern of a parent who denies dangers to the child. But it is still a clear and unambivalent "no." A woman said "I'd hate to have an adult walk in and hear the nonsense songs I sing to my son. One day after lunch I found myself having to wash his face. He *hates* being washed. So I did this operatic farce and playfully insisted on what had to be done:

"O.K. Charlie time to wash the squash from your face.
Here comes the washcloth."
  "No!" "No!" "No!"
  "No! No!, wash the squash."
  "No, we wash a lot."
  "No, squish, No, squash."
  "No, mish, no mash."
  "Behold Charlie! I can see your shining face again!"

Because "no" has gotten such a bad press, parents
often fear that "no" is associated with "being a witch,"
being stingy, or withholding. This mixed feeling creates
ambivalence in a parent's tone of voice when they have
to say "no."

Another mother said, "I hate saying 'no' to my children so much. I know how important it is not to be
ambivalent, so I drown out my wish to say '*yes*' only to
find myself barking my "no" like a crack drill sergeant.
Then I forbid them to react to me with disappointment
or dismay. I just don't want to hear about it."

But that is what a mature parent needs, the ability to
say "no" and accept the angry disappointment of a de-
nied youngster. If the "no" has been unambivalent, chil-

dren will know it, and the disappointment will probably be short-lived. If they detect a glimmer of ambivalence or mixed feelings in your voice, they will play their anger and disappointment to the hilt to see if they can drive a wedge into your denial.

For certain children it is difficult to know if your "no" is final. They hear your "no" as if it had been whispered from across the Grand Canyon. For them, you must express your "no" as intensely as is needed so there is no doubt that you mean what you say. When you really don't know if you need a "no" or a "yes" in a given situation, it's perfectly correct to delay the answer with an honest, "You know, I'm not sure, let me think about it, and I'll tell you by such-and-such a time."

Adults have difficulty saying "no" to each other, too. They fear engaging the finality of "no." They'll whip up a froth of angry commentary that leads to nothing when what they really want to say is "no." Even among themselves, adults must learn to give a "no" honestly and clearly and accept "no," perhaps not joyfully but certainly as a reality.

A wife will contract the proverbial headache rather than say "no" to her husband's sexual wishes. She actually takes on pain in her fear of giving pain. She defines her husband as too weak to fully engage her current reality and deals him a blow by not allowing him the chance to be strong enough to hear her clear and honest "no."

"No" as a word is "worse" than "yes" only when used disproportionately. "No" has rights equal to "yes."

"Opposites attract," they say, but be that as it may, parents often juggle their feelings and attitudes between themselves early on in a marriage where one partner takes on a general pessimistic attitude and the other partner upholds the positive. Indeed, between themselves they balance and augment each other's viewpoints and responses. But eventually that balance ceases to work. The pessimist, for instance, can become so unrealistic and negative that the optimist leaps too quickly to a positive position that is equally unrealistic. The two have developed a gap in the middle and their true values fall through the gap and get lost. The two no longer help each other as partners but only react to each other. Living only "one role" can eventually become divisive.

> A woman says, "I hate riding the broom in my house all the time! My husband is so positive and permissive with the kids without seeming to consider the prices or possible consequences of his generous permission. That makes me feel first, aced out of an equal share in the decision making process. Second, I feel bereft of the opportunity to be the positive and giving person I used to see myself as being. And, third, I get stuck with the consequences and the follow-through of his generous gestures because I'm with the children more than he is. Now the kids go to him for his inevitable 'Yes's' and I've become the witch who doles out 'No's.' Saturday he took them out for ice cream, not knowing that I had already told them that we were going to have to wash the car together.

Here "no" has become the sole right of one partner and "yes" the privilege of the other. As each person in the partnership wants to grow to a balanced and responsible wholeness within himself or herself, they feel uncomfortable bearing only one side of the message. Trading seats on the seesaw is not a long-term solution, although initially trading places may be necessary to wrench themselves out of the habits or patterns the couple has already formed. Whenever one partner is enlightened and ready for a new developmental step toward wholeness and takes some first steps in that direction, the balance between partners becomes shaky and precarious. That's not bad, but it is unsettling and often painful.

The mother speaking above needs to see why she's been so comfortable riding that broom of hers for so long. She has every right to pick up the whole tab and speak from her deepest self—stating a "yes" or a "no"—and not just reacting to her husband out of a need to make balance. She needs to talk this out with her spouse and tell him how she feels. She needs to be clear enough to know her own mind. She might create some "*yes* is the answer" situations artificially for awhile just to park her broom in the corner for a time and practice the joys of saying "yes" to her youngsters. Her husband might check out his motives to see if he fears saying "no" because he is not strong enough to withstand his youngsters' disappointments or some bouts with "unpopularity."

The tensions between "*yes*" and "*no*" are superseded when each partner knows himself clearly enough to speak out both answers with authenticity, joy, and authority.

The One-Minute Scolding is a great arena for both parents to grapple with and express positive and negative realities fully and wholly. If "no" is the word a two-year-old uses with the daring of one who has discovered his key to autonomy, then "no" or a fascination for the forbidden is a major issue once again in adolescence.

When parents grapple with the two sides of the truth in a two-year-old's emancipatory gesture, they recognize that "no" is a healthy child's attempt to separate. They acknowledge and applaud the child's separation but at the same time they protect him from "delusions of grandeur." Children must not leap from the role of helpless babe to almighty dictator! The successful accomplishments of "the terrible twos" will stand one in good stead when emancipatory efforts of adolescence appear some years later.

Another factor that plays an important part in parenting a teenager is just how well the parent survived his/her own adolescence. How much autonomy did the parent attain at that time?

Consciousness and clarity are again imperative in saying "yes" or "no." Goals and values must be clear: say what you mean and mean what you say.

> "Mother may I go out to swim?"
>
> "Yes, my darling daughter. Hang your clothes on the hickory limb, but don't go near the water."
>
> This mother says "yes," but means "no."
>
> A mother tells her fifteen-year-old daughter, "You may not sleep with your boyfriend, but if you are going to I'll put you on the pill." Or, if she forbids her daughter to have sexual intercourse with her boyfriend but does not set clear guidelines about when to be home, how often they may go out, and does not enforce these limits clearly, firmly, and lovingly, then she has said "no," but means "yes."

The story of the forbidden fruit in the Garden of Eden deals with the problem of "no." This is a paradigm of the emancipation issue. Every paradise has its forbidden fruit. At first one is forbidden the fruit but by adolescence one is faced with the serpent itself. Eventually one eats of the fruit and tastes as never before "the knowledge of good and evil." This knowledge casts us from the bliss of ignorance into another reality. Here enter the tensions of knowing good from evil, the problem of choosing for ourselves between "yes" and "no." Guilt and vulnerability, shouldered and accepted, allow us to pick up our bags and walk into adulthood, choosing between the two, paying the prices incurred by this choice, and experiencing the joys offered by that choice. God himself says in effect, "You blew it, but I love you and I'm going to help you."

Deep down, parents sense that it is ultimately necessary for their children to disobey that "no" in order to emancipate. Saying "no" to one's parents is an act of emancipation. Small wonder that "no" is filled with such feeling and ambivalence. It represents both freedom for our children and the loss of them.

Our children's emancipation will succeed only when the rules and values we have imparted to them have been clear and firm enough to push off from. Emancipation will succeed only when the child is mature enough to cope with the consequences of his choice. Hence parents must create a formative setting for their children in such a way that they can obey until they are strong enough to disobey. Children not given this firm and loving parenting will not be equipped with the strength, maturity, and the trust in humankind to emancipate successfully. They will "camp outside the gates" of paradise longing for lost innocence and unable to pick up and engage their humanity.

10 Asking Common Questions, Avoiding Common Mistakes

After being introduced to the One-Minute Scolding or after using it for a time, some parents encounter circumstances or responses that cause them difficulties. We pass along these experiences, both good and bad, to help in understanding what does and what does not work. This sampling of questions has come from parents and teachers and will help to clarify the scolding for you.

Q: What if I use the One-Minute Scolding and it doesn't work? When my child continues to misbehave, what do I do?

A: The first thing you must ask yourself is, "Am I giving the whole One-Minute Scolding, or am I administering only part of it? Am I giving it the prescribed way?"

One mother who has been using the scolding with real success for a year told me that she had caught herself scolding her son one night and wondered why it wasn't working. She was preparing some snacks for guests who were about to arrive and was rather involved in the process. Her little fellow kept coming out of bed to see if the guests had arrived yet, and might he help chop this or that, and chattering about nothing. Well, she wanted him off and in bed. It was late, and he had had a story and his usual nighttime rituals. So she told him to hustle back to bed and go to sleep—now! When he padded out to kitchen for the fifth time, she realized that things weren't working.

She told me that then she washed her hands and reviewed her tactics, only to discover she'd indeed given her message about getting back to bed, but she had not taken enough time to convey how seriously she felt about this, and how really annoyed she was with his reappearances.

Second, she had not taken enough time with the second half of the scolding either! Her son felt only shunted off, not loved or good about himself.

Third, she had forgotten to touch or hold or hug him because of her greasy fingers. She told me that as soon as she had done the One-Minute Scolding completely and properly with all of its parts and in the right order and had touched and held him, it was over. He scurried right off and went to bed.

This mother's experience is quite typical. When you use the One-Minute Scolding properly, it works. If you find that the One-Minute Scolding isn't working, you may find it very useful to review the last chapter and look at the structure of the scolding itself. Be sure that you use it entirely and correctly.

Q: My child is tough. What should I do when she shows no signs of feeling upset? Should I go on expressing my anger until she does?

A: No. The first half of the scolding should last no more than thirty seconds. You are not going to solve all your disciplinary problems with some children in the first thirty seconds. Most children need several scoldings until a change occurs. But each scolding should be kept within the prescribed time limit.

Q: During the first half of the scolding, if my child cries right away do I still have to go on and on with the scolding?

A: When you see that your child is feeling *upset*, you have scolded him enough. It is not how long you scold your child (although it should *never* be longer than half-a-minute), but rather how clearly you scold him and how intensely you express your real feelings during the scolding that count. You want your child to feel your sadness, your anger, your annoyance, your frustration, and/or whatever feeling you have about his misbehavior.

Probably better than anyone else, you know when your child is having feelings. From the slight changes in his facial expression, a tightness around his mouth, a sad look or tears in his eyes, or perhaps the drooping of his head, you can detect the changes in his feelings. As soon as you see that your boy is feeling upset, stop. You have given him your message and the first half of the One-Minute Scolding is over.

Q: Why shouldn't I use additional punishments along with the One-Minute Scolding? Wouldn't that work faster?

A: No. It isn't necessary and it doesn't work. Punishment in any form tends to elicit anger and resentment from your children and this interferes with their learning new and acceptable behaviors. Discipline such as the One-Minute Scolding may also be very uncomfortable for your child, but your intention is to teach rather than to hurt. Your child will feel the difference and respond accordingly.

Q: Are you saying that the only discipline that I need to use with my child is a scolding?

A: Yes. One of the advantages of the scolding method is that when it is over, it is over. It is less work and it is more effective. Natural consequences should be allowed to happen if they are not hurtful, because they teach your child as well. You may want to discuss the matter further, but more in terms of exploring his or your feelings as well as helping you and your child gain more information so as to handle that particular situation in a more mature and adaptive manner.

Q: What if I feel only slightly annoyed with my child, but think that I will make a greater impact on her if I am angry? Should I try to act angry during the first part of scolding?

A: No. Express only what you really feel. Don't role-play. Your honest feelings will make a much stronger impression on your child. They know. Remember, the scolding is more than a disciplinary method; it is a means of communicating with your child, and of developing a better relationship with a child, a relationship that is based on truth and trust. After the fact, your child will remember your honesty and will continue to trust you. The more honest you are as a parent, the more successful you will be with your children.

Q: What should I do if I feel I've just made a big mistake in trying to discipline one of my children? Let's say that I have sent my child away and I refused to talk to her?

A: I think it is very useful for parents to make mistakes. It provides them with a wonderful opportunity to teach their children how to deal with their mistakes.

As soon as you realize you've made a mistake, go to your child and say, "I'm sorry. I made a mistake. Instead of helping you with your problem, I sent you away and refused to talk to you. Will you forgive me?"

You will be surprised and touched at how readily your

child responds in a loving and forgiving manner. Your willingness to admit to a mistake and ask forgiveness will not be forgotten and you may well hear your words and actions return to you in the following weeks.

Q: I really have trouble seeing myself going home and using this idea because it feels like "the answer." I figure my kids will soon catch on to it as a pat formula that needs to be tuned out.

A: You are right. The One-Minute Scolding has a prescribed formula that is a big hurdle at first for many people. It makes them feel controlled, as if their own creativity is being suppressed.

When we teach people how to use the One-Minute Scolding, we *are* teaching an answer. Just as teaching children the times-table is teaching "the answers," the ritualized approach of the One-Minute Scolding assures us that we have all the parts necessary to get to the best answer. It doesn't leave you with any blank spaces. The balance is inherent in the ritual and produces a true and effective answer. It's a good ritual because all of the parts are there. You don't have to run around finding the right pieces. That's already been done. It works whether you understand it or not. But there is no doubt at all that you'll like it better when you "know it in your bones." Then you have made it your own. When you see how it works and appreciate it, you'll be very creative in your interactions with your children. Then you will be able to keep your feeling expressions balanced without feeling like you are using a formula.

Q: I find it difficult to stop scolding after only thirty seconds and act warm and loving when I am still very angry. Isn't that being hypocritical?

A: Many people ask that question as they learn to use the scolding. Remember, we use adult skills and strengths to express anger adaptively and to stop expressing negative feelings at the end of thirty seconds. This is challenging but relatively easy to learn with practice. At the end of those first angry thirty seconds or less take that deep breath and remind yourself that you do not stop loving your child when you are angry and upset with her. You're not lying to her when you express your love in the second half of the scolding. You do love her. You *do* know that she is a good person. You know she will learn other ways of behaving. You know that you'll never stop being her parent. Her behavior or your anger do not make her a bad person or an unloved child. You're angry and upset at her *behavior*, not her person. That's not hypocritical, that is maturity.

Q: Won't my expression of anger frighten my daughter and cause her to bottle up her own feelings?

A: Most parents can safely express the full force of their anger to their children without harming them. Fathers probably should "hold back" a bit as their anger seems more frightening and overwhelming to children. Most mothers when using the scolding can give full vent to their rage without overwhelming their older children. Obviously, infants and small children cannot cope with the full expression of adult anger.

Using the scolding gives parents a way of expressing anger in a mature and helpful way. It is also a way of teaching children how to express anger. One mother adds this example. She is a social worker who helps other parents learn how to use the One-Minute Scolding but when using it personally gave the following example:

> "When we adopted Lisa, a five-year-old Korean orphan girl, I began to use the scolding in my own home. She was having trouble adjusting and was misbehaving. Her behavior improved considerably and I really have not had

to use it much in the last few years. But I think that the biggest payoff has been what it has taught her about herself.

"Unfortunately, my husband and I are divorcing and things have been difficult for all of us. But in the middle of this trying time, I couldn't help but smile when my daughter came up to me and said, 'Mother, I am angry. You and daddy are getting divorced. It's not fair. I am very angry!' I could almost hear myself over the years saying, 'Lisa, I am angry. You did such and such . . . and I am angry!'

"As much as it hurt me to see her so upset I was pleased to see that my daughter wasn't holding back the way I did when I was a child. I know that since I've started to use the scolding to express my own feelings that I feel much better about myself and about her."

Q: What if I do not discipline my child every time she misbehaves? If I am inconsistent will the One-Minute Scolding still work for me?

A: The more consistent you are, the better behaved your child will be and the better your relationship will be. Use the One-Minute Scolding as often as you can when your child misbehaves. But don't worry about it when you don't. Remember, the One-Minute Scolding isn't asking for "perfection," it is asking for your best effort. It is better for your daughter if you do scold her every time she makes a mistake. But sometimes it is just impossible for you to even spend that one moment. Give yourself a break. The One-Minute Scolding is designed to make parenting easier, not more difficult.

Q: How important is it for me, as a father, to get involved with the discipline? Can I leave it up to my wife because she is better at this sort of thing anyway?

A: Many men have a difficult time expressing feelings, especially the warm and tender feelings.

The One-Minute Scolding is almost as important for the father as it is for his youngsters who need to be disciplined. The One-Minute Scolding allows parents to practice both feelings, the angry, annoyed, and irritated ones as well as the warm and loving feelings. Although parents may feel a bit clumsy and embarrassed at using the One-Minute Scolding in the beginning, they will find that the scolding is a way for them to practice expressing themselves fully, completely, as well as appropriately.

"Wait until your father gets home" is fortunately a dying expression in households today. We are purging ourselves of some of those old stereotypes of tough dad/ soft mom roles. But in many cases, we've only reversed them. Now we are seeing tough mothers/soft fathers, and that won't work either. So the One-Minute Scolding is like practicing scales on the piano. You practice the right hand and the left hand. It's no longer seen as excusable to leave the other scales for someone else to play.

If the mother jumps in and tries to balance out the father, she'll deprive the dad of a complete expression of feelings and deprive him of the opportunity to develop a close, warm relationship with his children. We all tend to be at least a little lopsided in our abilities to express feelings. That's why the One-Minute Scolding is a great exercise for parents. You may be clumsy at first, but it will teach you balance. It is also very important for children, both boys and girls, to hear their dads express feelings and express them honestly, completely, and appropriately. Parents need to encourage each other to keep practicing.

Q: Should I warn my child first before I actually give her a scolding? Should I give her another chance?

A: No. Either scold your child when she misbehaves, or don't scold your child. A threat only suggests that you may, in fact, not scold your child for the misbehavior that has already occurred.

Q: What if someone tells me that my child has misbehaved, should I give him a scolding?

A: No. Scold him for misbehaviors that you've observed or that you are very certain have occurred. However, it is important that you talk to your child about the misbehavior that's been reported to you. This gives you as a parent a good opportunity to help your child deal with the problem that occurred outside of the home.

Q: What if my child needs to tell me something during the scolding? Isn't it important for children to express their feelings and for parents to listen to them?

A: During the scolding it is important that you do not get drawn into a discussion. It is a scolding, not a discussion. There is a proper time and place for listening to your child, but the middle of the scolding is neither the time nor the place. After you have finished and given him a hug or a loving touch, encourage him to express his feelings or discuss the pertinent issues. Then it is important to listen carefully and with respect. Encourage his discharge of feeling so that the two of you are at peace with one another. Don't get caught in a verbal war or argument. If he expresses his feelings inappropriately, he is not necessarily misbehaving. Remember, you are the adult, so you can cope with his feelings in a mature manner.

Q: I thought my child's feelings were the most important thing?

A: Feelings are important. Helping your child express feelings in an appropriate manner is equally important.

Frustrating the wishes of a child for her own good is a loving gesture that parents can make.

Don't mix up wishes, whims, or power-plays with feelings. If you give into a child's every wish you do not help him learn to deal with reality. The outside world is not so indulgent.

Q: How does this method of discipline compare with behavior modification, which I have been reading about, where the child is disciplined (or taught) by having to experience the consequences of her own action?

A: The One-Minute Scolding is compatible with behavior modification. One of the unpleasant consequences of your daughter's misbehavior may be the scolding she gets from you. You can, of course, also let her experience the other natural consequences of her actions.

If your son leaves his bike out on the lawn, despite repeated warnings that it will be stolen if he doesn't put it into the garage, you can give him an understanding response when his bicycle is stolen but good discipline includes pointing out to him the consequences of his misbehavior. Your child does not need a scolding or any other kind of discipline because he will feel very upset about losing his bike. If you try to scold or discipline him further, your child loses the beneficial experience of "natural consequences." He has lost his bicycle and must replace it.

Q: What if I used the method but my husband doesn't? Will it still work?

A: Yes. One parent using the One-Minute Scolding consistently is better than neither parent scolding the child effectively. However, it is far better if each parent is supporting the other by using the same method of discipline.

A child is in a serious situation if one or both parents undermines the other when disciplining the child.

Single parents who use the One-Minute Scolding effectively prove their ability to raise a youngster without a partner, even if it would be easier and more effective to have two parents participate. Separated parents should agree on common rules and limits as well as using a discipline familiar to all. This reduces the tensions and troubles that arise out of children living in different homes with separated parents.

Q: Can I use the One-Minute Scolding in public places or is it better to wait until we get home?

A: Let's say your youngster misbehaves in the supermarket. The supermarket is actually a great place to use the One-Minute Scolding. Back him up against the canned goods, nose-to-nose, whispering intensely and glaring angrily into his little eyes.

After fifteen to twenty seconds of hissed scolding, most children are very relieved to have you relax and smile. Use the scolding consistently and he will behave well in public places, supermarkets, or restaurants. Remember that it is the certainty of discipline that prevents misbehavior.

Q: What should I do if my child misbehaves when it really is inconvenient to discipline her at that moment?

A: You are the parent and you have the power to decide when and where you discipline your child. If it is inconvenient to discipline her at the moment give her a look or tell her "I'll talk to you later about this," and forget it for the moment. However, it is important that you remember to discipline your child at a later date when it is more convenient.

However, the more often you choose not to discipline your child in a certain situation, the more likely you are to have a problem with your child in that circumstance. I know a parent who used the scolding very successfully with her child except in one area. Whenever she was on the phone, her three-year-old would misbehave. The child was taking advantage of the fact that her mom was preoccupied. The more important the phone call, the more likely it was the child would misbehave.

Suddenly the mother saw the light and she made an important change. The next time she was on the phone and her child began to misbehave, she interrupted her telephone conversation and said, "I'm sorry. My daughter needs my help. I'll call you right back, in fact in two minutes." She spent the next minute administering the complete scolding. There were a few more interrupted phone calls, but in a week the problem was over.

Q: I rarely need to use the One-Minute Scolding with my son anymore because he hardly ever misbehaves.

But I actually miss that chance it gave me for the *intense*, positive interaction which felt so good to me. What can I do to get that again?

A: That's a very important point. You'll have to create them. Fathers don't always have enough routine time to be around their kids as it is. You may want to make a special point of seeking out reasons to be positive and warm with your son by praising him for all those things he does well: answering the phone so nicely, picking up his room, even walking and looking well. Don't forget to just express how nice it feels for you to be his father. Physical expression of positive feelings intensify those words such as patting, holding, hugging, pinching, tugging, and tussling with your children.

There are some youngsters who find it particularly hard to respond to your positive feelings. They don't easily feel your love. I advise those parents to "pounce on your kid!" Children should be surprised and embraced in a big bear hug without warning but with warm, intense feelings of love and affection.

At first those kids think "Oh, oh, I've been found out." They fear that you've found out one of the many things they've done for which they should be scolded. So they actually interpret your surprising embrace as trouble. Imagine their relief and joy when you say, "I just wanted you to know how much I loved you."

Q: How can I use the principles of the One-Minute Scolding in my classroom? Do I want my students to bond to me as their teacher?

A: Look at it this way. Remember when you were a kid. Do you remember any adults or especially a teacher at school who thought you were a wonderful youngster? Remember one who liked you and you looked forward to being around her? Unfortunately for many youngsters, memories of pleasant adults will be rare. But those who have had such special adults are very grateful for them.

When a teacher takes even a few minutes to relate to each student personally and warmly and just as positively as she does negatively, she gives that child a gift that lasts a lifetime. Teachers, like parents, represent authority, security, warmth, nurture, and care, as well as information. When a teacher creates a secure place, free of worry and tension, she reduces anxiety for the student and in that way frees the student to learn.

Actually, attachments can form quickly between students and teachers. Teaching implies a kind of partnership. The processes of teaching and learning call forth a whole range of feelings on both sides of the partnership. If you praise and encourage and nurture the students, attachments form.

Kids who misbehave give their teacher an opportunity to form attachments to them because the teacher can employ a form of the One-Minute Scolding. It will be slightly different from the form parents use, but the essentials are the same.

> "Boris! Don't shoot spitballs in this class. I don't like it." Then touch him lightly on the shoulder and say, "I understand you get bored when you don't understand the problem. Tell me when you don't get it. I enjoy helping you."

Simply put, you form an attachment and enhance and facilitate learning. You yourself will have to endure the pain of loss each spring as your students move on. But you have made a great impact, giving a lasting gift to a youngster when you are willing to be understanding and helpful in a real way—truly present and not rejecting.

Q: My ten-year-old is very independent and rarely asks for my help. He is really quite grown-up and makes his own decisions most of the time. I can't imagine giving him a One-Minute Scolding because it would feel like I'm scolding another adult.

A: Your child pays a heavy price for an "independence" which appears to be so healthy and adult. Actually he is learning not to trust you to be present and helpful for him when he is in need. If he does not learn to trust you and turn to you for help, perceiving you as a loving parent, who can he trust? Such independent children usually grow up to be independent but also lonely and alienated adults who are unable to be intimate and trusting with anyone, including their spouses.

Such children are often born with an "independent" temperament and require unusual strength, consistency, and most important, intensity from their parents. These children require a prompt and intense scolding for each misdeed. Your expression of positive feelings must be very intense and physical so that your child can *feel* your love.

The degree of "independence" that you seem to be describing does not sound like a genuine independence at all, but more like a withdrawal or alienation. Indeed, we raise our children carefully and lovingly with their ultimate independence from us as a goal. They love to say, "Let me try it—let me do it all alone." Healthy children very naturally strive for autonomy. But it is a child's right to find healthy comfort as he proceeds in his development. It is not natural or healthy for a child to turn only to himself for solutions to problems. If a youngster turns inward and rarely reaches out for help or direction, especially when they are in trouble, it may mean that either 1) a loving, helpful, consistently present adult has not been available to them or the adults they know are too punitive to be trusted for help or they may be too weak or 2) the child may have been born with a "hard to reach" temperament.

Either of these conditions causes the youngster to be thrown against himself because he cannot or he will not trust that there is anybody out there who can really help in any way. Such lack of trust only causes intense loneliness and an inability to admit anyone into his real life. Eventually, if not corrected, it will cause an inability to trust even a spouse—an inability to share, to love, to feel, and to be vulnerable to others. He only feels an alienation and separation from life that allows him to indeed "fend for himself," but that is not the same as independence or autonomy.

Children with an "independent" temperament or orientation require unusual intensity of feeling from their parents. They need strong, consistent, and prompt input for misdeeds. Most important, the expression of positive feelings must also be very intense, penetrating, and even tangible. This is the only way to cure them of their distance and teach them trust. They must know that there really is someone who loves them unconditionally and helps them know right from wrong.

Q:　My child lies all the time. He's eight. He lies even when it isn't necessary for his protection. Will the One-Minute Scolding help him get over this habit?

A:　When children lie, parents get very upset and fear that this is an indication of a serious flaw of character. A child learns to lie when he feels he cannot trust his parents with the truth. Telling the truth only causes more trouble than he is already in and with no promise of a helpful or compassionate solution.

So when a child has misbehaved and you have very clear evidence of the problem, approach him in a way that shows him clearly that you are there to work this out and help him to a better solution. Do not put him on the spot by asking him questions which will give him a chance to lie and compromise and compound the problem. If you already know the answer, take it from there.

> Asking Billy if he ate the chocolate candy when his face is already decorated with evidence is daring him to lie. Scold him promptly with the One-Minute Scolding. If it turns out that you have made a mistake and it was only gravy on his chin, apologize sincerely and ask his forgiveness. It gives him a great feeling of being morally in the right for once.

Every chance you get, praise him warmly and intensely whenever he tells the truth. Define him as an honest child in every way you can—even in front of others. If he lies and doesn't live up to that definition of honesty, respond with your surprise and disappointment and then give him a One-Minute Scolding. The scolding states clearly your sorrow that he forgot you were going to help him and that he must trust you with the truth and have faith in your ability to handle the truth. In the positive half of the scolding, assure him that you'll always help him and that telling the truth makes it easier for you to help him. Promise that you'll scold him every time until he remembers not to lie and that you will only scold him and not lose control around him. Tell him that you love him very much and you know that he is a good fellow who really wants to be truthful.

Q: What should I do when I feel like I hate my child?

A: Hate is an extreme form of anger. Parents, all parents, get very angry at their children at different times and for different reasons. It is never helpful to tell your child that you hate him because it implies that there's something wrong with his very being. This usually occurs when problems have gone on for some time and you have been frustrated in trying to get your child to behave more appropriately.

Using the One-Minute Scolding every time your child misbehaves allows you to discharge your anger and frustration each time he misbehaves and also helps you to express those warm and loving feelings that most, if not all, parents feel for their children. The first few days or even weeks may require ten or fifteen scoldings a day, but that means only ten or fifteen minutes a day. After using the scolding for a period of time, you will find that the number of scoldings required drops off sharply, and that your child's behavior changes dramatically. Don't be discouraged. All parents feel overwhelmed with fear that they are not good parents. Use the One-Minute Scolding as a tool that will help you get back on the track.

Q: My neighbor has real problems disciplining her children. In fact, I classify her as an abusing parent. Would the One-Minute Scolding be helpful to her?

A: Abusing parents feel helpless in dealing with their lives as well as disciplining their children effectively and in a warm and loving manner. Your support and encouragement could be very helpful to her and her family. If you could develop a relationship with her so that she sees you as a helpful and wise neighbor she might allow you to teach her how to use the One-Minute Scolding.

Obviously the One-Minute Scolding leads to much happier results than physical and emotional abuse. In my experience, abusing parents have learned to use the One-Minute Scolding very quickly when they have not felt criticized and humiliated and embarrassed because of their troubles in disciplining their children. They are often very grateful and gratified by the results that come shortly after using the One-Minute Scolding.

Q: Can't this method of scolding be misused? Can't you batter children emotionally with such a scolding?

A: Any tool can be misused. The One-Minute Scolding is difficult to misuse if it is used properly. Parents find it impossible to continue screaming at their children after they have expressed their warmth and caring in a loving manner in the second half of the scolding. The scolding is not just for children. It is designed specifically to help parents be effective, loving parents.

Our problem has been to convince parents to use the scolding and to use it correctly. It has been our experience that parents who use the One-Minute Scolding never batter their children emotionally or psychologically.

Q: I have three or four foster children in my home at one time. I also have a son of my own. These foster children come and go all the time, visiting their mothers, returning, going to live with their fathers, etc. I notice that just before and just after one of these weekends away they really get naughty. Should I use the One-Minute Scolding with these children? Should I try to develop a relationship with these children? Should I use the One-Minute Scolding on my own child as well?

A: Foster mothers have used the One-Minute Scolding with remarkable success. Encouraged to develop a warm intense relationship with their foster children even though the children may be living with them for just a few weeks, foster parents can help these children thrive when they teach them how to behave and teach them values to live by. The One-Minute Scolding has proven to be invaluable to foster parents.

It is easy to use the One-Minute Scolding on your

own child as well as your foster children. The tactic is so simple and easy to use that it comes naturally after a few months of regular use. Your foster children will feel cared for as though they were your own and your own natural son will feel that he's fairly treated and not neglected by your attention to your foster children.

Q: I'm divorced. When my daughters go to their dad and stepmother's for the summer they live by different rules and they live a very different lifestyle. What's the use of doing the One-Minute Scolding, setting reasonable limits, and expecting them to behave properly when they get to do anything they want when they live with their father and stepmother?

A: This is a common problem and often a difficult one to resolve perfectly. However, you have your daughters most of the year and, since discipline is teaching, there's no reason whatsoever why you should feel you cannot teach your children proper behavior and the values that go with them while they live with you.

Children love to know how to behave and what values to live by. They will love you for disciplining them in a consistent and caring manner and despite their summers in an unstructured, unsupervised situation, nothing can take that from them. Children who are unsupervised and uncared for are sad, lonely, and angry kids. Perhaps if you approach your ex-husband in a positive and friendly manner he will cooperate in setting appropriate limits and disciplining them in a consistent manner.

Q: My two-year-old bites when he's angry and my mom told me that if we bite him back he'll learn fast what that feels like. Frankly, I can't imagine my talking about it would get through to him. Will the scolding work for my two-year-old?

A: Biting your two-year-old hard enough to make

him stop usually causes fear and mistrust in your child. As you know, a bite hurts a lot. Use the One-Minute Scolding instead. A two-year-old needs only a very short first half of the scolding, but it should be sharp and intense in response to his biting. A dramatic, loud *"no"* when he bites followed by reassuring warmth immediately afterwards will soon teach him not to bite. Try it for a few days. You will be delightfully surprised.

Q: Recently I saw my son misbehave while playing with his friends outside. I called him in to give him the One-Minute Scolding in private. But he became terribly upset with me because I wasn't going to let him explain his side of the story first. We got into a terrible argument and I ended up not scolding him, but sending him to his room. How should I have handled that?

A: Remember that discipline is teaching. If your son was so upset because of what had happened outside or because you had called him in from his play with his friends, he is not "ready" to be taught. Encourage him to express his anger, frustration, and resentment until he is ready to listen. This may take a few hours if he has learned that screaming and yelling at you will get him his way. However, if you will persist, remain calm, and responsive, he will eventually calm down and can be scolded.

Then proceed with the scolding, first reassuring him that it will take only a minute and that he can go out to play after you have finished the discipline. If he continues to protest, hear him out and then ask him if he is ready for his One-Minute Scolding. Obviously, he will be anxious to return to his play outside and will soon learn that if he "takes his medicine" it only takes a minute and he will then be free to return to his play.

Q: When I get angry and scold my boy and then right away hug him and praise him and tell him how much I love him, I feel like I'm pushing his feelings around. Isn't this confusing to a child?

A: At first it is. But after you have done it a few times he will come to expect and appreciate your disciplinary efforts. Your boy knows that you can be angry with him and also love him at the same time. Expressing those feelings, first anger and then abruptly switching to love and care, is a very effective way to teach him how to handle two strong conflicting feelings at the same time.

11 A Rapid Review of the One-Minute Scolding

This chapter is a rapid review of the One-Minute Scolding. Making major changes in your thinking is never easy. Breaking old habits takes time. The way you were scolded as a child and probably the way you've tried to discipline your own up until this frustrating point has been a part of you for years. So be patient with yourself as you change your punishments of the past into this better disciplinary technique, the One-Minute Scolding.

To help yourself make the changes you want and to get the results more quickly, this chapter was prepared as a quick review. Read it or scan it daily for the first month. You'll be pleased and surprised at how quickly you will be able to master the technique.

BEFORE I BEGIN THE SCOLDING

The One-Minute Scolding is a scolding, not a discussion.

I am the only one I will allow to talk during

the scolding. I will remind my child that he is being disciplined and that he may talk with me after the scolding.

The One-Minute Scolding is painful for my child.

He will try whatever it takes to get me to stop. He may laugh, look bored, interrupt, squirm away, or try a variety of other maneuvers to get me to stop using the One-Minute Scolding. But I love my child enough to continue to use the One Minute Scolding until he learns to behave himself and, in the process, to like himself.

No matter what happens, I complete the scolding.

For the One-Minute Scolding to be effective, I must do the entire scolding, regardless of circumstances. I will allow nothing to interfere with completing this process which is so important for my child's well-being.

THE FIRST HALF OF THE SCOLDING

I scold my child in private.

I do this because I do not want to humiliate my child in front of others and because I know that when my child and I are alone together, he is better able to concentrate on his misbehavior and how it affects our relationship.

I get in physical contact with my child.

Depending upon my child's age, I put him on my lap, or I put my arm around his shoulder, or I hold onto his forearm, or at least I have my fingertips on his shirt sleeves.

*I stay in physical contact with my child
for the next minute.*

My hand, face, and body communicate first my angry and disappointed feelings and then my warm and caring feelings directly to my child. He cannot "turn off" or hide from that communication.

I express my feelings in simple and clear language.

My child must understand the rule he has broken. So, I describe clearly the misbehavior or the broken rule that caused my anger. For example, "I am angry *because* you did X, Y, and Z. I get very angry when you do that."

I scold the behavior, not the child.

My children will tend to believe whatever I tell them repeatedly. Therefore, I avoid saying things like, "You are bad," or, "You are stupid." Instead, I scold the behavior: "You behaved badly," or, "That was a thoughtless thing to do."

I express how angry or upset I am.

I want my child to learn to understand and express feelings. I say, "I am so angry that I want to spank you." In this way, I am teaching my child *how* to deal with strong feelings and, by example, *how not* to deal with strong feelings, such as hitting, retreating, or feeling hurt.

*I communicate my feelings with my body language,
tone of voice, facial expression, as well as
with the words that I use.*

Words, body language, facial expressions, must all be congruous and thus not confuse my child as to the message being sent. Otherwise, I will not be effectively teaching my child the good behavior I want him to learn.

I continue to express my feelings about
my child's behavior until I see that
my child feels my anger or disappointment.

I will know this when I see a change in mood (tears, facial expressions, trembling lip, etc.). My child feels that this misbehavior has upset me. She, too, is in a state of excitability. This tells me the first half of the scolding is over.

I keep my scolding brief.

I realize that I may have a great deal of unexpressed anger that I would like to vent. However, I know that if I prolong my scolding or make it too intense, my child can "tune out" or get too worried and not learn what I want to teach. I do not try to get all of my feelings out in one scolding.

THE SECOND HALF OF THE SCOLDING

I take a few deep breaths and remind myself
how important my child is to me.

I have my child's full attention. Now, I want him to be flooded with my warmth and caring.

I abruptly change to a tone of voice, facial expression,
and body language that is warm and caring.

I have told my child what I am angry about, how angry and upset I am, and now I must communicate my love and concern for my child in a clear and consistent manner. This rewards the child for listening.

I express my love and concern for my child.

Again, I use simple language. "You are a good boy. I know you want to behave. I want to be a good parent and I'm going to help you." My tone of voice, my touch, and my facial expression all must be consistent with the words that I use.

I validate my child as a person of importance and integrity.

I tell her that she is a good person. I tell her that I want her to grow up to be a good, strong, healthy woman. I tell her that she's a good person and a person of value.

I remind my child that when she misbehaves, I scold her.

I tell her, "I am scolding you because you misbehaved. I care for you so much that I am going to scold you every time you make a mistake like that." I tell her that if she breaks the rule again, I will scold her again.

I tell my child that it is easy to scold her.

Discipline need not be a hardship nor something to be avoided. I love my child. I scold my child because I love her. I want my child to feel certain strength and maturity. My child will be relieved if I can discipline her in a simple, effective manner, and consistently.

I reassure my child that whenever she breaks a rule and needs discipline, I will be there to give her the discipline she needs.

"Every time you blow it, I'm going to scold you because I love you. It's no big deal for me. I like to be a good, strong parent. So I'll scold you every time you make a mistake. It's easy for me."

THE CONCLUSION OF THE SCOLDING

Did my child learn what I wanted him to learn?

I want to be effective. I want to know if my child learned the lesson of the moment. So I ask, "Why am I scolding you now?" I wait for an answer. If he doesn't know, it means that either he doesn't want to tell me, or that my scolding has been too vigorous and his fear and anxiety have flooded him and interfered with the learning of that which I wanted to teach. So I tell him, "I'm scolding you because you hit your sister."

I ask him why I scold him every time he misbehaves.

"Now, why do I scold you every time you blow it?" I want him to respond with, "Because you love me." If he doesn't recall, I tell him again, "I love you." Or, if I find it difficult to express such intense positive feelings for my child, I may say, "I care for you very much."

I end a scolding by hugging or touching my child.

The hug tells him that I love him and the scolding is over. An older adolescent may only allow me to pat him on the shoulder or on the arm. This sign of affection is the signal I have finished the discipline.

After I have scolded my child.

When the scolding is over, it's over! I do not mention it again. I do not ask my spouse to scold him again. We may want to discuss the matter, but there will be no more scoldings. One scolding is enough.

*I encourage my child to do whatever she wishes
after the scolding.*

My child may choose to stay near me or to go off by herself to think about things.

*I encourage my child to express her feelings
at this time.*

My child may be angry or sad and may want to talk about her feelings. I encourage her and listen patiently. She may tell me that she doesn't think the scolding was fair. She may tell me that she is angry and upset with me for scolding her. I listen to her carefully. I hear her out and, unless I am proved wrong later, I do not apologize, nor do I make excuses for disciplining her. I disciplined her because I love her.

She may not want to talk about her feelings immediately, but she may want to do so later. This I should support and encourage.

12 | A Scolding Diary

For your convenience, we have prepared a Scolding Diary which you can use to record your progress.

In the column labeled, "Comments," it is important for you to note any special difficulties and/or successes you have experienced. This will help you to identify patterns and areas of weakness as well as to congratulate yourself on your successes.

If you are a typical parent, you may find yourself initially scolding your child as frequently as five to ten times each day. This should consume from five to ten minutes of your day. Very shortly, you should note a dramatic decrease in the number of scoldings necessary each day. Of course, for children with special difficulties, the reduction in frequency will be slower.

Most parents tend to forget to use the One-Minute Scolding when the need becomes less frequent. Therefore, we urge you to continue to use the diary for an extended period of time so that this disciplinary strategy truly becomes second nature for both child and parent. In the proper circumstances, both will intuitively feel that something is missing if the scolding is not used.

Scolding Diary		
Date	Time (AM/PM)	Comments
		(Significant difficulties, successes, and breakthroughs)

(On the bottom of each page, the following questions should also be asked:)
1) Did I limit the scolding to one minute?
2) Did my child understand clearly what the issue was?
3) Did I scold the behavior and love the child?

Bibliography

Babcock, Dorothy and Keepers, Terry. *Raising Kids OK*. New York: Grove Press, 1976.

Bach, George, and Goldberg, Herb. *Creative Aggression: The Art of Assertive Living*. New York: Avon, 1975.

Biller, Henry, and Meredith, Dennis. *Father Power*. New York: David McKay, 1974.

Bowlby, John. *Maternal Care and Mental Health*. Geneva: World Health Organization, 1951.

———. *Child Care and the Growth of Love*. Harmondsworth, England: Penguin, 1965.

———. *Attachment and Loss*, Vols. I, II, III. New York: Basic Books, 1973–1980.

———. "The Making and Breaking of Affectional Bonds: Aetiology and Psychopathology in Light of Attachment Theory," *British Journal of Psychiatry* 130 (1977):201–210.

Branden, Nathaniel. *The Psychology of Self-Esteem*. New York: Bantam, 1971.

———. *Breaking Away*. New York: Bantam, 1972.

Brazelton, T.B., et al. *Parent-Infant Interaction*, Ciba Foundation Symposium 33. New York: Elsevier, 1975.

Briggs, Dorothy Corkille. *Your Child's Self-Esteem*. Garden City: Doubleday, 1975.

Coopersmith, Stanley. *The Antecendents of Self-Esteem*. San Francisco: W.H. Freeman, 1967.

Dobson, James. *Dare to Discipline*. New York: Bantam, 1970.

———. *Emotions: Can You Trust Them?* Glendale, CA: Regal, 1980.

Dodson, Fitzhugh. *How to Parent*. Los Angeles: Nash, 1970.

———. *How to Discipline with Love*. New York: Rawson Associates, 1977.

Dunn, Judy. *Distress and Comfort*. Fontana: Open Books, 1977.

Eisenberg, L. "The Fathers of Autistic Children," *American Journal of Orthopsychiatry* (1957): 715–725.

Eriksen, Erik. *Childhood and Society*. New York: W.W. Norton, 1950.

———. "Identity and the Life Cycle," *Psychological Issues* (monograph), Vol. I, No. 1, 68.

Farmer, Bill. "No Paddle Ball in Sweden," *Parade* (March 16, 1980).

Freud, Anna. *Beyond the Best Interests of the Child*. New York: The Free Press, MacMillan, 1973.

———, and Burlingham, Dorothy. *Infants Without Families*. New York: International Universities Press, 1973.

Friedman, Robert, et. al. "Parent Power: A Holding Technique in the Treatment of Omnipotent Children," *International Journal of Family Counseling*, 68073.

Ginnot, Hiam. *Between Parent and Child*. New York: MacMillan, 1965.

Glueck, E.T., and Glueck, Sheldon. "Identification of Potential Delinquents at Two to Three Years of Age," *International Journal of Social Psychiatry* (1966).

Greenberg, Martin, and Morris, Normal. "Engrossment: The Newborn's Impact Upon the Father," *American Journal of Orthopsychiatry* 44/4 (July 1974).

Howell, Mary C. "Employed Mothers and Their Families," *Pediatrics* 52/3 (September 1973):14.

James, Muriel. *What Do We Do With Them Now That We've Got Them?* Reading, Mass.: Addison-Wesley, 1974.

———, and Jongeward, Dorothy. *Born to Win: Transactional Analysis with Gestalt Experiments*. New York: Signet, 1978.

Johnson, Thomas. "Guidelines for Discipline," published by the Youth Service Bureau and the San Diego County Probation Department.

Kempe, Ruth S., and Kempe, C. Henry. *Child Abuse*. Fontana: Open Books, 1977.

Klaus, Marshall H. and Kennell, John H. *Maternal-Infant Bonding*. St. Louis: C.V. Mosby, 1976.

Kohlberg, L. *Stages in the Development of Moral Thought and Action*. New York: Holt, Rinehart, and Winston, 1969.

Kotelchuck, Multon. "The Nature of the Child's Ties to His Father," unpublished Ph.D. dissertation, Harvard University, Boston, April 1972.

————, et al. "Infantile Reaction to Parental Separation When Left Alone with Familiar and Unfamiliar Adults," *Journal of Genetic Psychology* 126 (1975).

————, et al. "Separation Protest in Infants in Home and Laboratory," *Developmental Psychology* 11 (1975).

————, et al. "Father Interaction and Separation Protest," Developmental Psychology 9 (1973).

Lamb, Michael. "Proximity Seeking Attachment Behaviors: A Critical Review of the Literature," *Genetic Psychology Monographs* (1976).

Levine, James A. *Who Will Raise the Children: New Options for Father (And Mothers)*. New York: J.B. Lippincott, 1976.

Lowen, Alexander. *The Language of the Body*. New York: MacMillan, 1971.

————. *Bioenergetics*. New York: Penguin, 1976.

Maslow, Abraham. *Towards A Psychology of Being*. New York: D. Van Nostrand, 1962.

Mitchell, Gary; Redican, William; and Gomber, Jody. "Lessons from a Primate: Males Can Raise Babies," *Psychology Today* (April 1974).

Parker, Ross and O'Leary, Sandra. "Father-Mother-Infant Interaction in the Newborn: Some Findings, Some Observations, and Some Unresolved Issues," in K. Riegel and J. Meachem, eds., *The Developing Individual in a Changing World*, Vol. II. The Hague: Norton, 1975.

Redican, William, and Mitchell, Gary. "Play Between Adult Male and Infant Rhesus Monkeys," *American Zoology* 14 (1974).

Restak, Richard. "The Origins of Violence," *Saturday Review* (May 12, 1979).

————. *The Brain: The Last Frontier*. New York: Doubleday, 1979.

Rogers, Carl. *On Becoming A Person*. Boston: Houghton Mifflin, 1961.

Rutter, Michael. *Maternal Deprivation Reassessed.* Middlesex, England: Penguin, 1972.

Salk, Lee. *What Every Child Would Like His Parents To Know.* New York: David McKay, 1975.

Satir, Virginia. *Peoplemaking.* Palo Alto: Science and Behavior Books, 1972.

"Saving the Family," *Newsweek Magazine,* Special Report (May 15, 1978).

Schaffer, Rudolph. *Mothering.* Fontana: Open Books, 1977.

Scharlatt, Elizabeth, et al. *Kids: Day In and Day Out.* New York: Simon and Schuster, 1979.

Schutz, Will. *Profound Simplicity.* New York: Bantam, 1980.

Seay, B., Alexander, B.K., and Harlow, H.F. "Maternal Behavior of Socially Deprived Rhesus Monkeys," *Journal of Abnormal and Social Psychology* 69/4 (1964):347.

Silberman, Melvin and Wheelan, Susan. *How To Discipline Without Feeling Guilty.* New York: Hawthorn, 1980.

The Bible (King James Version), Proverbs 23:24.

Toffler, Alvin. *Future Shock.* New York: Random, 1970.

Van Buren, Abigail. "Dear Abby," *The San Diego Union* (May 2, 1979).

Viscott, David. *How To Live With Another Person.* New York: Arbor House, 1974.